J. Haykin

A COMMONSENSE APPROACH TO THE
THEORY OF ERROR CORRECTING CODES

A COMMONSENSE APPROACH TO THE THEORY OF ERROR CORRECTING CODES

BENJAMIN ARAZI

The MIT Press
Cambridge, Massachusetts
London, England

Publisher's Note

This format is intended to reduce the cost of publishing certain works in book form and to shorten the gap between editorial preparation and final publication. Detailed editing and composition have been avoided by photographing the text of this book directly from the author's prepared copy.

This book was printed and bound in the United States of America.

Library of Congress Cataloging-in-Publication Data

Arazi, Benjamin.
  A commonsense approach to the theory of error correcting codes

  p.   cm. — (MIT Press series in computer systems)
Includes index.
ISBN 0-262-01098-4
1. Error correcting codes (Information theory) I. Title. II. Series.
TK5105.5.A7 1987   005-72—dc19   87-21889

This book is gratefully dedicated to J. H. J. Filter in recognition of his inspiring guidance through the initial phases of my research career

CONTENTS

PREFACE

Applying error correction and detection techniques when transmitting or storing binary data has become a vital issue. Computer networks, on the one hand, and compact disks, on the other, demonstrate the scope of the field in which error correction and detection codes are used.

Teaching the theory of error correcting codes on an introductory level is very difficult. The theory, which has immediate applications, concerns abstract algebraic concepts such as finite fields and primitive polynomials. Such concepts, which are usually dealt with within the first few chapters of standard textbooks, simply scare students off.

The originality of the material presented in this book lies in the new way in which the entire issue of error correcting codes is treated. Based on the author's ten years experience in teaching this subject, all the fundamental concepts of error correcting codes are explained in terms of exclusive-OR (XOR) gates, linear feedback shift registers, and basic techniques from linear algebra (nothing beyond a simple vector-matrix multiplication). Using this commonsense approach, the author was able to cover a wide range of single error correction block-codes without referring at all to the complex algebraic terms mentioned above. Diffuse-threshold- decoding convolutional codes were selected for presenting this kind of codes.

Those readers interested in an advanced algebraic introduction to error correction theory can refer to the appendix. There the basic principles discussed throughout the text are re-examined from a more theoretical angle, where finite field arithmetic is introduced. This algebraic treatment is given however only after the student has already gained an intuitive understanding of what is happening. The material presented can be covered in a one-semester undergraduate course in electrical engineering or computer science. It can also be used as an introductory review in more advanced courses, for it forms an easy-to-understand basis, from which the rest of the material can build.

A COMMONSENSE APPROACH TO THE
THEORY OF ERROR CORRECTING CODES

CHAPTER 1
INTRODUCTION

1.1 A Communication System and the Effect of Errors

This book is concerned with the transmission of binary digits, known as **bits,** from a source known as the **transmitter** to a destination known as the **receiver**. On their way from the transmitter to the receiver these bits pass through a medium known as **channel**. While in the channel the bits are subject to noise which introduces errors in the sense that some received bits have a value opposite to that of the corresponding transmitted ones.

Unless specified otherwise, we are concerned here with bits that are transmitted in blocks of a fixed length. It is assumed that no bits are inserted into a block or omitted from a block during transmission. It is also assumed that there is always block synchronization (i.e., the receiver always knows where one block ends and another begins).

The system depicted in Fig. 1.1 treats a block of length 7. The transmitted block is 1001101 and the received one is 1100101. The received block differs from the transmitted one in the bits located at the second and fourth place, counting from the left. (These bits are 0 and 1 in the transmitted block and 1 and 0 in the received one.)

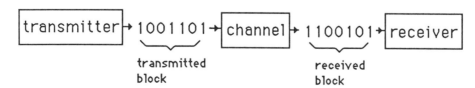

Fig. 1.1 A communication system

Before continuing, the reader should be reminded of the XOR operation, well known from logic design. **This operation is denoted throughout the entire text by +** (which usually denotes an OR operation). We then have

$$0 + 0 = 0, \ 0 + 1 = 1, \ 1 + 0 = 1, \ 1 + 1 = 0$$

Observe that if a + b = c, then a + c = b, and b + c = a. This observation, stating that it is possible to transfer elements from one side of an equation to the other while still keeping the + sign, is proved simply by noting that if a + b = c, then by adding "a" to both sides of the equation we have that a + a + b = a + c. Since a + a = 0, by definition, then b = a + c. This property, which is used rigorously in this text, also means that whenever we have to perform a subtraction (e.g., during a division operation), we can perform an addition instead.

An XOR operation can be summarized by saying that XORing a bit x with a 0 yields a bit with value x, and XORing it with a 1 yields a bit with value x', where x' denotes the complement of x.

The sum of two blocks of bits (both of the same length) is the result obtained by XORing bitwise the two blocks. The result is itself a block of the same length as each of the two addends. (Its first element is the result obtained by XORing the first elements of the two blocks. Its second element is the result obtained by XORing the second element of both blocks, etc.) The resultant block then has a value 1 in those places where the two blocks differ and value 0 in the places where they have the same value.

As an example, consider the two blocks 1100110 and 1010101. These blocks differ in the second, third, sixth, and seventh places. Their sum is 0110011.

Definition   If A is a transmitted block and B denotes its received version, then the block A + B is **the error pattern block**.

Note that A and B differ in those places where an error has been introduced by the channel. Their sum, which has a value 1 in the places where the blocks differ, is therefore a block whose 1 elements indicate the location of errors. Note also that if E = A + B, then B = A + E, meaning that the received message is obtained by adding the error pattern block to the transmitted code word.

As an example that clarifies the above definition, consider the transmitted and received blocks depicted in Fig. 1.1. These blocks are 1001101 and 1100101, respectively. Their sum is 0101000. It has elements of value 1 in the second and fourth places, which are the locations of the errors.

1.2 The Concept of Parity

The parity of an integer can be either odd or even. It can be denoted by a numerical value as defined next.

Definition   An even parity is called **parity 0**. An odd parity is called **parity 1**. (Odd numbers then have parity 1, and the even numbers have parity 0.)

One can also talk about **the parity of a certain group of bits** which refers to the parity of the number of elements of value 1 in the group. As an illustration, consider the block 11001011. The parity of the first four elements of the block is 0. The parity of the last four elements of the block is 1. The parity of the entire block is 1.

A basic property, needed for further use, is: *The parity of the sum of two blocks equals the sum of their parities.* That is, if A and B are two blocks whose sum is C, where the parity of these blocks is a, b, c, respectively, then c = a + b. (Note that a, b, c are *bits*.)

Next we consider the possibility of calculating the parity of a given group of bits using standard logic gates. A gate that serves this purpose is a multiple input XOR gate. By definition, the output of such a gate indicates the parity of the group of bits that forms its input. For example, take the case of a seven-input XOR gate. If exactly 6 of the inputs have value 1, the output is 0. If exactly 3 of the inputs have value 1, the output is 1. Fig. 1.2 illustrates how a multiple input XOR gate is constructed from standard two-input gates, with the output being the parity of the input group.

A basic operation commonly used in this text is the conversion of a block of bits of length k into a block of length k + 1 having a parity 0. Such a conversion is based on the following simple principle. If the number of 1 elements in a block of length k is odd, then by attaching to this block a bit of value 1, we form a block of length k + 1 having an even number of 1's. On the other hand, if the number of 1 elements in the block is even, then by attaching to it a bit of value 0, we finish with a

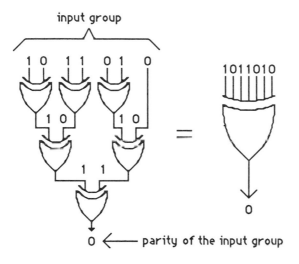

Fig. 1.2 A multiple input XOR gate

block of length k + 1 having an even number of 1's. This observation can be stated as follows. A block of k bits can be converted into a block of k + 1 bits having parity 0 by attaching to the original block a bit whose value equals the parity of this block. This parity bit is obtained by XORing all the k bits of the original block. Fig. 1.3 depicts the described process.

1.3 Error Detection

The purpose of transmitting a binary block is to convey some information from the transmitter to the receiver. It is generally assumed here that the receiver has no prior knowldge of the contents of the block transmitted to him. This means that if the transmitter wishes

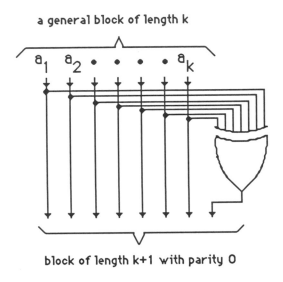

a general block of length k

block of length k+1 with parity 0

Fig. 1.3   Converting a block of length k into a block of length k+1 having parity 0

to transmit a random pattern of k bits, and the transmitted block consists only of these k bits, the receiver cannot have any idea as to whether any errors were introduced into the block on its way to him (since he expects some unknown k bits and he receives some k bits). In order to enable the receiver to determine whether a received block contains some errors, the block needs some properties whose violation indicate that the block has been changed on its way to the receiver. The existence of such properties would mean that the receiver knows something about the transmitted message, even though it contains random information. This could be done by attaching extra bits to the k information bits at the transmitter before transmission, thereby extending the k information bits into a block of length n, where n > k. The extra bits would be redundant as far as the information content of the message is concerned (the information content of the message is still the random pattern of k bits). They are needed so that the receiver may determine whether a received block of length n, for n > k, contains errors. The act of deciding whether a received block contains errors is called **error detection.**

It should be made clear at this stage that there is no way of *always* being able to detect whether a received block is in error. There are always some error patterns whose existence in a received block cannot be detected. Note also that detecting the existence of errors does not mean that the receiver knows anything about the nature of the errors (e.g., how many are there or where are they located). *Error detection simply means that the receiver detects the fact that that some errors exist in a received block,* and it therefore does not equal the transmitted one.

We demonstrate next a basic way of detecting the existence of an odd number of errors in a received block. As was shown before, it is possible to convert any block of length k into a block of length k + 1 having a parity 0, by attaching to the original block a bit that equals the parity of the block. Consider now the case where an information block of length k is to be transmitted. Before the actual transmission takes place, let the transmitter attach to this block its parity bit, thus converting it into a block of length n = k + 1 having parity 0. The receiver knows that any transmitted block (of length k+1) has parity 0. Upon receiving a block, the receiver checks its parity , and the received block is determined to have errors if and only if its parity is 1. Fig. 1.4 depicts the described scheme. The process performed at the transmitting end, where an information block I is converted into a

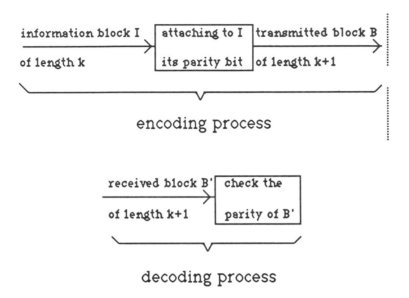

Fig. 1.4 A basic error detection scheme

transmitted block B, is called an **encoding process**. The process performed at the receiving end, where the received block B' is checked for errors, is the **decoding process.** Note that the received block does not have the same notation as the transmitted one.   B' is the received version of B and does not necessarily equal B due to the effect of errors.

Let us now analyze the performance of this error detection scheme (i.e. we wish to see which errors can be detected and which cannot). Let B' = B + E, where E is the error pattern block. The parity of B is 0. The receiver checks whether B' has parity 0. As was already stated before, the parity of the sum of two blocks equals the sum of their parities. This means that B' will have parity 1 (in which case errors are detected) if and only if E has parity 1. Since every element of value 1 in E indicates an error, it follows that by applying our scheme *we can detect the existence of an odd number of errors.*

We can conclude that by expanding k information bits into a transmitted block of length $n = k + 1$ having parity 0, and by checking the parity of the received block, it is possible to detect the existence of an odd number of errors and impossible to detect the existence of an even number of errors.

1.4 The Concept of Block Codes

A **block code** will mean here a collection of binary blocks, called **"code words"**, all of the same length. The terms "binary block", "binary vector" and "binary word" are freely interchanged depending on the context in which they are used. Table 1.1 lists the code words of a certain code.

The code of Table 1.1 consists of the collection of all the blocks of length 4 having parity 0. Each such block is a code word and there are altogether 8 code words in the code. These were constructed by selecting all possible binary blocks of length 3 and then attaching to each block its parity bit. As was discussed before, if a transmitter transmits

0000	1001
0011	1010
0101	1100
0110	1111

Table 1.1 An example of a code

only code words belonging to this code, and this fact is known to the receiver, it is possible to detect the existence of an odd number of errors in a received block.

Each code word of length n in a block code is generally constructed by expanding an information vector of length k. The expansion is done by attaching to the information vector **parity bits,** whose values are calculated from the information bits. The number of code words in a code is therefore determined by the possible number of random selection of k bits. This number is 2^k. In the code of Table 1.1, k = 3 and n = 4, and the number of code words is 2^3.

Notation **An (n, k) block code** is a code in which each code word is of length n, of which k bits are information bits. (The number of parity bits is therefore n − k.)

The code described in Table 1.1 is a (4, 3) block code. We have not yet referred to the location of the k information bits within a code word. These bits can be located anywhere within the code word, and they do not have to appear successively. A block code in which the information bits are grouped together is called a **systematic block code.** Note, however, that for a given code, the information bits are located in the same places in all the code words.

1.5   Review of the Concepts Introduced

It is vital that the reader be very familiar with all the concepts listed below before continuing with the text.

Binary *block* , binary *vector*, binary *word* : All refer to a string of bits having a specified length.

Sum of two binary blocks: The block obtained by XORing two blocks (of the same length) element by element.

Error pattern block: A block having the 1 elements in those places where a transmitted block and its received version differ.

Binary blocks with parity 0: A binary block having an even number of elements of value 1.   (This includes the case where a block has no elements of value 1.)

Binary block with parity 1: A binary block having an odd number of elements of value 1.
(Important observation: The parity of a block is the sum of its bits.)

Error detection: The process of determining at the receiving end whether a received message is erroneous.

Binary block code: A collection of binary blocks of the same length.

Code word: A binary block belonging to a given block code.

Information content of a code word: The number of bits in a code word that can be selected randomly.

(n, k) block code: A block code having code words of length n, of which k bits are information bits. The information bits form the data to be protected against errors. (The rest of the n − k bits are the 'parity bits', calculated as a function of the information bits. Their purpose is forming the possibility for correcting errors.)

Systematic block code: A block code in which the information bits are grouped together within a code word.

CHAPTER 2
LINEAR CODES

2.1 Basic Concepts

Definition **A linear code** is a code in which the sum of any two code words is also a code word. (The way of summing up two binary blocks has already been defined in section 1.1.)

We illustrate this by considering the code listed in Table 1.1. The sum of any two code words out of the eight is still a block within these eight blocks.

Definition **The Hamming weight** of a binary block is the number of elements of value 1 in it.

Definition **The Hamming distance** between two binary blocks (the two must be of the same length) is the number of places in which they differ.

Example The blocks (1010111) and (1111010) both have Hamming weight 5. They differ in the second, fourth, fifth, and seventh places. Altogether they differ in four places, and their Hamming distance is then 4.

As was shown earlier, the sum of two blocks A and B is a block C having elements of value 1 in those places where the two blocks A and B differ. The number of 1 elements in C is therefore the Hamming distance between A and B. This number, on the other hand, is the *Hamming weight of C*. We then have that the Hamming *weight* of the sum of two binary blocks is the Hamming *distance* between these two blocks.

Definition   The **minimum Hamming distance** of a code is the minimum result obtained by measuring the distance between all possible pairs of the code words. The **minimum Hamming weight** of a code is the minimum result obtained by measuring the Hamming weight of all the code words, excluding the code word consisting only of 0's (should it exist).

Example   The minimum Hamming distance of the code of eight code words demonstrated in Table 1.1 is 2, since any two words differ in at least 2 places. The minimum Hamming weight is also 2.

An important observation is that *in a linear code, the minimum Hamming weight equals the minimum Hamming distance.* This is shown by first observing that the "all 0" block must be a code word since the sum of any code word with itself which must belong to the code (based on the linearity definition) yields an all 0 word. If A is a code word having the minimum Hamming weight d, then the minimum Hamming *distance* between A and the "all 0" block is also d. It is impossible to have two other code words, say B and D, having a distance e less than d. If this were the case, then C + D, which is also a code word, would have weight e, which contradicts the fact that d is the minimum weight.

The only block codes with which we are concerned in this book are linear codes.

2.2 *Minimum Hamming Distance of a Code and the Error Detection/Correction Capability of the Code*

Take the case where a vector $A = (10110011)$ is transmitted. The vector is subject to errors on its way to the receiver, where the errors are characterized by the error pattern $E = (11001001)$. The received vector B is then $A + E - (01111010)$. The number of errors that occurred in A on its way to the receiver is 4, which is the Hamming weight of E. This number is also the Hamming distance between A and its received version B. We can generally say that the Hamming distance between a transmitted vector and its received version is the Hamming weight of the error pattern.

Suppose that a transmitter and a receiver have a list of code words of a specific code and they agree that any block conveyed between them must be one of these code words. Upon receiving a message, the receiver will decide whether errors exist in this message by checking whether it is a code word of the code. If it is, he will decide that no errors have occurred. If the received message is not a code word, he will decide that the message is erroneous.

Definition The **error detection capability** of a code is the maximum number of errors that can occur in a transmitted code word and that will still *always* enable the receiver to detect the fact that a received message is erroneous. (Such a detection is made by observing that the received message is not a code word.)

We now show a connection between the error detection capability of a code and its minimum Hamming distance. Let us denote the minimum Hamming distance by D(min). This means that any two code words of the code differ in at least D(min) places. Suppose now that we transmit a code word A that is received as a vector B. If errors have occurred - and B therefore does not equal A - the only way of *not* being able to detect this fact is if B is another code word, since error detection is based on checking whether B is *any* code word. Note that this observation shows that no matter how many parity bits are attached to an information vector, it is impossible to construct a code in which the existence of errors in a received message is *always* detected (unless the "code" consists of a single code word). This is due to the fact that there is always a possibility that a transmitted code word A is received as another code word B, and that the errors were not detected.

Conclusion 2.1   Errors are not detected in a received message if and only if the error pattern vector is in itself a code word.

In order to see why this conclusion is valid, take the case discussed before where a code word A is received as another code word B (which is the only case under which errors are not detected). Let $E = A + B$. Due to the linearity of the code, the error pattern E is also a code word, which validates the conclusion.

Conclusion 2.1 also forms the basis for calculating the probability of not detecting errors. Many reliable communication systems are based only on error detection, in the sense that a received message is checked for errors. If errors are detected (i.e., it is detected that the received message is not a code word), a retransmission of the message is requested, and the retransmitted message is checked again for errors, etc., until a message is received with undetected errors. It is important to calculate the probability of not detecting errors in order to analyze the performance of the system. For a linear code, this probabilty is the probability that the error pattern vector will be a code word.

Let us see now what is the minimum number of errors that have to occur in a transmitted code word A for it to be received as another code word (in which case error detection is impossible). Since D(min) is the minimum number of places in which A differs from any other code word, this means that at least D(min) errors must occur in A during transmission in order for it to be received as another code word B. On the other hand, if the number of errors occurring in A is D(min) − 1 or less, the occurrence of errors will always be detected because the number of errors is insufficient to convert A into another code word.

Conclusion 2.2 The error detection capability of a code is D(min) − 1, where D(min) denotes the minimum Hamming distance of the code.

We next consider the possibility of *correcting* errors in a received message, knowing that the transmitted message was a code word. Correcting errors in a message means recovering the location of the erroneous bits after detecting that the received message is erroneous (i.e., detecting that a received message is not a code word). The corrected message should equal a code word in the code used by the transmitter and the receiver.

Definition   The **error correction capability** of a code is the maximum number of errors that can occur in a transmitted code word under which it is still *always* possible for the receiver to recover the original message.

We demonstrate the evaluation of error correction capability of a code by first considering an example. Take the case where the transmitted code word A is 11001100, the received message M is 11111100, and another code word B (in the code used by the transmitter and the receiver) is 11111111. The Hamming distance between A and M is 2. This is also the distance between B and M. Suppose you are given M, and someone tells you that there are two errors in it, as compared to its transmitted version which was a valid code word. It is impossible for you to determine whether the transmitted code word was A or B, since M can be obtained by introducing two errors either in A or B (and maybe in some other code words whose Hamming distance from M is 2). It then follows that the error correction capability of the code is less than 2.

The preceding example can be looked upon from a different angle. The Hamming distance between A and B is 4. The message M lies exactly in the middle between A and B (its distance is 2 from both code words). It is therefore impossible to determine the original version. *Error correction is therefore possible only if the number of errors is less than half the minimum Hamming distance of the code* because this will ensure that an erroneous received message will be closer to the code word that it was originally than to any other code word. The error correction capability of a code is then the largest number that is smaller

than D(min)/2. This number is [(D(min) − 1)/2], where the   square
brackets denote the integer part of the number, for example, [1] = 1 and
[1.5] = 1.

Conclusion 2.3   The error correction capability of a code is
[(D(min) − 1)/2].

   In view of conclusions 2.2 and 2.3 the error detection/ correction
capability of a code depends on its minimum Hamming distance. The
higher the minimum Hamming distance, the higher is the error detection
and correction capability. The same result also means that if a code
enables the correction of up to t errors in a code word, then the minimum
Hamming distance of the code is at least 2t + 1.

   We can now summarize the idea behind the possibility of devising
error detection/correction codes. The minimum Hamming distance of a
(k, k) code consisting of all the 2^k random vectors of length k is 1.
Parity bits can then be attached to each of these vectors, for the purpose
of increasing the minimum Hamming distance. These parity bits are
calculated from the random bits. By attaching more and more parity
bits, it is possible to increase the minimum Hamming distance of the
code, keeping the number of code words fixed.   This process is
demonstrated in Table 2.1.

   Column (a) of Table 2.1 lists all the patterns of 4 bits.   The
minimum Hamming distance here is 1. Column (b) is obtained by
attaching an extra parity bit, forming code words with parity 0. The
minimum Hamming distance here is 2. Column (c) is obtained by

0000	1000	00000	10001	0000000	1000110
0001	1001	00011	10010	0001101	1001011
0010	1010	00101	10100	0010111	1010001
0011	1011	00110	10111	0011010	1011100
0100	1100	01001	11000	0100011	1100101
0101	1101	01010	11011	0101110	1101000
0110	1110	01100	11101	0110100	1110010
0111	1111	01111	11110	0111001	1111111
(a)		(b)		(c)	

Table 2.1   Increasing the minimum Hamming distance of a
code by attaching parity bits

attaching three parity bits to the words of the first code. The minimum
Hamming distance here is 3. The way this code was constructed will be
explained in the next section. (Do not be misled. In order to achieve a
minimum Hamming distance 3, it is not always sufficient to attach
only 3 parity bits to the initial k random bits.)

2.3   Hamming Codes

It is possible to generate a code with minimum Hamming distance 3
whose code words are of length $2^m - 1$ for any given m, where each
code word consists of $2^m - m - 1$ information bits and m parity bits.
It is also known that this code is the most efficient when considering
the number of parity bits needed to be attached to an information
vector in order to achieve a minimum Hamming distance 3. This efficient

code is called a **Hamming code**. Possible dimensions for Hamming codes are then (7, 4), (15, 11), (31,26), etc.

Since a Hamming code has a D(min) = 3, its error detection capability is 2, and its error correction capability is 1.

There are various ways of constructing a Hamming code. (Constructing a code means converting information vectors of length k into code words of length n, by attaching to an information vector n − k parity bits which are calculated from the information bits.) Each such construction will yield a different code. For example, the code in column (c) of Table 2.1 is a (7, 4) Hamming code. Table 2.2 lists another (7, 4) Hamming code.

The code in Table 2.2 was constructed in the following way: An information vector of length k = 4, whose general form is (a, b, c, d), was converted into a code word of length 7 by attaching three parity bits denoted by p0, p1, p2. The information bits and the parity bits are located in the corresponding code word as follows: p0 p1 a p2 b c d.

0000000	1110000
1101001	0011001
0101010	1011010
1000011	0110011
1001100	0111100
0100101	1010101
1100110	0010110
0001111	1111111

Table 2.2 A (7, 4) Hamming code

The parity bits are calculated from the information bits in a way that satisfies the following equations:

(1) $p2 + b + c + d = 0$
(2) $p1 + a + c + d = 0$
(3) $p0 + a + b + d = 0$

(Recall from Chapter 1 that + means XOR).

In view of what we already discussed, the above three equations can be written as: $p2 = b + c + d$, $p1 = a + c + d$, $p0 = a + b + d$.

The list of the 16 code words in Table 2.2 was constructed by selecting all 16 possible information vectors of length 4 (all possible forms of a, b, c, d) and attaching to each such vector three parity bits, satisfying the above three equations, where the location of the bits in each code word is according to the order p0 p1 a p2 b c d. A circuit that converts an information vector into a code word, according to this process, is depicted in Fig. 2.1.

Definition **Encoding** is the process performed at the transmitter, where parity bits are calculated and attached to an information vector (thus forming the transmitted code word). The circuit performing the encoding is the **encoder**.

It can be shown that the code words of Table 2.2 are the only ones that satisfy equations (1), (2), and (3). This fact is very important. For example, a binary vector of length 7 can be checked if it is a code word of this code by simply checking if it satisfies equations (1), (2),

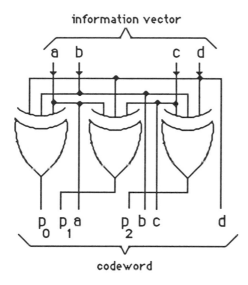

Fig. 2.1 Generating a code word from an information vector

and (3). In other words, the vector $D = (p, q, r, s, t, u, v)$ is a code word of the code of Table 2.2 if and only if $s + t + u + v = 0$, $q + r + u + v = 0$, and $p + r + t + v = 0$.

Fig. 2.2 depicts a circuit for determining whether or not a vector D is a code word of our code.

The outputs $y1$, $y2$, $y3$ of the circuit depicted in Fig. 2.2 are all 0 if and only if the vector is a code word from the code of Table 2.2.

Up to this stage we have not yet shown that the minimum Hamming distance of the code of Table 2.2 is 3. This can, of course, be verified by measuring the Hamming distance between all possible pairs of code words in the list of code words of this code.

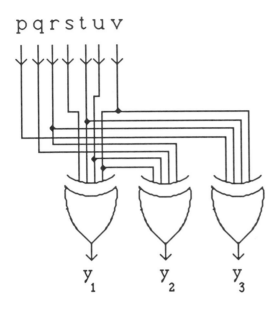

p q r s t u v

Fig. 2.2   Checking whether a vector is a code word of the code
            of Table 2.2

However, for tutorial purposes our aim is to prove this property by considering the error detection/correction capability of the code.

Let A be a transmitted code word, and let M be its received version. The receiver will try to detect whether errors have occurred during the transmission by checking whether equations (1), (2), and (3) hold for M. If they hold, then M is a code word. We now show how to correct a single error occurring in A (i.e., M differs from A in one bit). The bits of A are p0 p1 a p2 b c d, satisfying equations (1), (2), and (3). Let the corresponding bits of the received message M be (p, q, r, s, t, u, v). One of the bits in M is the complement of the corresponding bit in A, with the rest of the bits being those of A.

Erroneous bit in M	Respective values of y1 y2 y3
p	001
q	010
r	011
s	100
t	101
u	110
v	111

Table 2.3 The effect of a single error in M on the values of y1, y2, y3

Table 2.3 summarizes the effect of any single error in M, by listing the values of y1, y2, y3 generated by the erroneous M.

Note that each of the seven possibilities of having a single error in M has a different effect on the values of y1, y2, y3. This means that based on y1, y2, y3, it is possible to know which bit is erroneous in the case one error occurred. The case of no error is indicated by (y1 y2 y3) = (000). It follows that the error correction capability of the code is at least 1.

We show next that the error correction capability of the code is not more than 1. (The final aim of this tutorial discussion is to find D(min).) Consider, for example, the case where bits p and q in M are both erroneous. Entering M into the circuit of Fig. 2.2 we get $y_1 = 0$, $y_2 = 1$, $y_3 = 1$. From Table 2.3 it is seen that a single error in r will yield the same values of y_1, y_2, y_3. This means that it is impossible for the receiver to detect whether a single error or a double error occurred in M. The error correction capability of the code is therefore 1, and from what was discussed above, D(min) is either 3 or 4.

We now show that D(min) is 3 and not 4, by considering the error *detection* capability of the code. Take the case where bits p, q, r in M are erroneous and the rest are error free. In this case the reader can verify that equations (1), (2), and (3) will all hold (i.e., $y_1 = y_2 = y_3 = 0$), so no error detection will occur; this also means that M is a valid code word. Since we have demonstrated that the occurrence of three errors is not always detected, the error detection capability of the code is less than 3. We then have that D(min) - whose value is one more than the error detection capability - is less than 4. Since from the error *correction* capability of the code it has been shown that D(min) is either 3 or 4, it follows now that D(min) = 3.

There is an important point related to error correction/detection codes that must be clarified. Considering the code of Table 2.2 and the notations of Fig. 2.2, it was already shown that a single error in r and a double error in both p and q will yield the same y_1, y_2, y_3. There are numerous other error behaviors that will yield the same y_1, y_2, y_3. A valid question is: How can the receiver know that only a single error has occurred, before applying a single error correction procedure? The answer is that *the receiver really does not know the nature of the errors.* A decision on which kind of error correction procedure should be applied is based on prior measurements of the error behavior of the communication channel. The assumption that single errors occur is justified only after extensive statistical measurements have established this fact. Whenever this assumption is violated, the error "correction" will introduce a further error.

We have proved that D(min) of the code listed in Table 2.2 is 3. We have not proved that the same holds for the code of Table 2.1, column c, which is also a Hamming code, and we have not proved this property for a Hamming code with (n, k) values other than (7, 4). We also have not shown how to construct such Hamming codes. This and further work will be covered in the next sections.

2.4   The Parity Matrix of a Linear Code

2.4.1 Parity Matrix and Parity Equations
Notation Throughout the rest of this chapter the matrix denoted by **H** is specifically the one below:

$$
H = \begin{array}{ccc}
0 & 0 & 1 \\
0 & 1 & 0 \\
0 & 1 & 1 \\
1 & 0 & 0 \\
1 & 0 & 1 \\
1 & 1 & 0 \\
1 & 1 & 1
\end{array}
$$

Let X be a seven bit vector, X = (a, b, c, d, e, f, g). We then have:

$$X \cdot H = (d + e + f + g, \ b + c + f + g, \ a + c + e + g)$$

(The + denotes an XOR operation, and X ·H is therefore a binary vector.)

Note now the code listed in Table 2.2. The code word Z = (p, q, r, s, t, u, v) satisfies the following equations:

(1) s + t + u + v = 0, (2) q + r + u + v = 0, (3) p + r + t + v = 0

We can then say that Z·H = (0, 0, 0). Also any vector Y satisfying the condition Y ·H = (0, 0, 0) must be a code word of this code. The columns of the matrix H then form the coefficients of the equations that the code words of this Hamming code should satisfy. (The first column says that the sum of the last four elements of a code word should be 0, etc.) For a general (n, k) linear code there are n − k independent equations, based upon which the n − k parity bits are calculated. We can thus form for any general code a matrix whose columns are the coefficients of these independent equations.

Definition **The parity matrix** of a linear (n, k) code has n rows and n − k columns. Each column consists of the coefficients of one of the n − k independent equations that a code word should satisfy.

2.4.2 The Location of the Parity Bits in a Code Word as Reflected in the Structure of the Parity Matrix

If each parity bit in a code word of a code is calculated independently, it means that each of the equations from which the parity bits are calculated contains one and only one parity bit. Since the number of these equations is the number of parity bits, this last statement also means that each parity bit appears once in the complete set of the equations. This argument is clarified by considering again, for example, the three equations, from which the three parity bits of the (7, 4) Hamming code, treated in the preceding section, are calculated:

(1) $p2 + b + c + d = 0$

(2) $p1 + a + c + d = 0$

(3) $p0 + a + b + d = 0$

We observe next how the fact that each parity bit appears once is reflected in the parity matrix. As we have already stated, each column of this matrix represents the coefficients of each of the parity check equations. If each parity bit appears only in one equation, this means that there will be only one column in the parity matrix, which has a 1 in a location corresponding to that of a parity bit. This is clarified by observing the parity matrix H of our code. A code word corresponding to this matrix has the general structure p0 p1 a p2 b c d, where the columns of H represent the coefficients of equations (1), (2), and (3) stated above. The location of the parity bits in a code word is first, second, and fourth (counting from the left). Observe, on the other hand, that the first, second, and fourth rows of H contain only a single element of value 1. To summarize, if each parity bit is calculated independently based only on the values of some information bits, then the rows of the parity matrix, whose location is that of a parity bit in a code word, have a single element of value 1.

If the rows of such a parity matrix are ordered according to the binary representations of successive numbers, starting with the binary representation of 1 (which is the case with our matrix H), then the location of the rows with a single 1, which is also the location of the parity bits in a code word, is a power of 2. (Since the binary representation of a power of 2 has a single 1.) This explains why the parity bits in a code word of our Hamming code are specifically in places #1, #2, and #4.

2.4.3 The Error Correction Procedure of a Hamming Code as Reflected in Its Parity Matrix

The matrix H is the parity matrix of the code of Table 2.2. This code is a Hamming code enabling a single error correction and double error detection. Let us see now how this property follows from parity matrix considerations. Let X be a code word from Table 2.2, where X is transmitted and is received as a message Y. The vector $Z = X + Y$ is then the error pattern. We can also write $Y = X + Z$. For error correction/detection purposes the receiver takes the vector Y and multiplies it by H. We then have $Y \cdot H = (X + Z) \cdot H = X \cdot H + Z \cdot H$. Note that the vector $X \cdot H$ is all 0 since X is a code word, and therefore $Y \cdot H = Z \cdot H$.

Definition   Let X be a transmitted code word, and let Y be its received version. The vector obtained by multiplying Y by the parity matrix of the code is called **the error syndrome**.

Since $Y \cdot H = Z \cdot H$, it follows that *the error syndrome equals the vector obtained by multiplying the error pattern vector by the parity matrix*. Calculating the error syndrome is the first step in the error correction/detection procedure performed at the receiver.

Definition   **Decoding** is the process performed at the receiver, where the error syndrome is first calculated from the received message, and based on it, error correction/detection is performed. The circuit performing this operation is the **decoder**.

Observe now what happens if only a single error occurred in X on its way to the receiver. We find here that Z has a single element of value 1 whose location is that of the erroneous bit, while the rest of its elements are 0. The error syndrome Y·H, calculated by the receiver, was shown above to equal Z·H, which equals a single row in H whose location (counting from the top) is that of the single bit in Z. Since this location is that of the erroneous bit, we conclude that the error syndrome Y·H calculated by the receiver equals that row in H whose location is that of the erroneous bit. Since all the rows of H are distinct, a given error syndrome then enables us to identify uniquely the location of a single error. Note that in the specific case of the matrix H, recovering the location of a single error in Y from the syndrome Y·H is especially easy since the rows of H are the natural binary representation of the numbers 1, 2, 3, 4, 5, 6, 7 arranged in increasing order. It then follows that *for the code whose parity matrix is H, the syndrome equals the binary representation of the error location index.*

Example   Let the transmitted code word X be 0011001. Let Z = 0100000. The received vector Y is then 0111001, and the reader can calculate that Y·H = Z·H = (010). This syndrome is the binary representation of 2, which is the location index of the error (second from the left).

2.4.4 The Error Detection Procedure of a Hamming Code as Reflected in Its Parity Matrix

Let us see now how to use the properties of H in order to show that it is impossible to correct two errors that occur in the transmitted code word X. In this case the error pattern vector Z has two elements of value 1, with the rest being 0. The syndrome Y·H calculated by the receiver, which equals Z·H, then equals the sum of two rows in H whose locations are those of the errors. In order to be able to correct the two errors, we must have a way of telling what are the two rows whose sum yields the given syndrome. However, given any syndrome, there are a number of pairs of rows whose sum yields this syndrome. This means that it is impossible to determine from a given syndrome which were the two specific rows of H summed by the operation Z·H that yield this syndrome, and error correction is impossible. Also, the sum of two rows B and C in H always yields a vector D which is also a row in H. It is therefore impossible to tell from a given syndrome whether a single error has occurred (in which case the syndrome indicates the location index of the error) or a double error (in which case the syndrome equals the sum of two rows in H). This illustrates again what we have stated, namely, error correction is possible only if the receiver acts under the assumption that the number of errors in a received message does not exceed the error correction capability of the code.

Example   Let Y·H = Z·H = (100). The following pairs of rows of H are all summed to (100): (first, fifth), (second, sixth), (third, seventh). This means that for all the following z, the operation Z·H yields (100): Z = (1000100), Z = (0100010), Z = (0010001). Also a single error in the fourth place in y yields the same syndrome.

We show now how the error detection capability of the code of Table 2.2 is determined by observing the properties of H. A received message Y is determined to be erroneous if and only if the syndrome Y·H is not all 0. (Which indicates that Y is not a code word.) For Y containing a single error, we showed that Y·H equals a certain row in H. For Y containing two errors, we showed that Y·H equals the sum of two rows in H. We claim that such a sum can never yield an all 0 vector, ensuring detection. This follows from the fact that all the rows of H are distinct, and it is impossible that the sum of two distinct rows will yield an all 0 vector. If Y contains three errors then Y·H equals the sum of three rows in H. Since it is possible to select three rows from H whose sum is 0, error detection is impossible here. We can conclude that the error detection capability of the code of Table 2.2 is 2.

The error correction/detection capability of a code can then be determined from its parity matrix P as follows. The error correction capability of a code is t if all the different sums of t rows or less (but at least 1) from P yield different results, and there is more than one set of t + 1 rows from P whose sum yields the same result. The error detection capability of a code is r if it is impossible to find r or less rows in P whose sum is 0, where there are some r + 1 rows in P whose sum is 0.

We have now two different explanations on the possibility of implementing error detection/correction codes. One explanation, given previously, used intuitively Dmin (minimum Hamming distance) considerations. On the other hand, we just showed above how this possibility is viewed through the parity matrix P. We now show why these two aspects are identical, by proving very simply the following:

a) The minimum number of rows that can be selected from P such that their sum will yield 0, is Dmin.

b) All possible sums of [(Dmin-1)/2] or less rows from P yield different results, where [(Dmin-1)/2] is the maximum value under which this property exists.

Proof of a: If Dmin is the minimum Hamming distance of a linear code, then we showed that Dmin is also the minimum Hamming weight of the code. That is, any code word Vi of the code, except for the all 0 word, has a Hamming weight Wi of at least Dmin. Only the code words Vi have the property that Vi·P = 0. Note now that a multiplication of Vi by P means summing Wi rows of P. To conclude, it is impossible to sum less than Dmin rows of P such that their sum is all 0. On the other hand, take the code word V whose weight is Dmin. Since V·P = 0, we are able to find Dmin rows from P whose sum is 0.

Proof of b: Suppose we were able to find two sets of rows from P such that the number of rows in each set does not exceed [(Dmin-1)/2] and the sum of the rows from each set yields the same result. It then follows that summing the rows from both sets altogether, yields the result 0. We were then able to select less than Dmin rows from P whose sum is 0, which contradicts the preceding proof. It then follows that two such sets do not exist. Proving the second part of b is now obvious.

2.5   *Constructing a General Hamming Code*

We have conveniently treated the (7, 4) Hamming codes up to now. However, a Hamming code is generally a $(2^n - 1, 2^n - n - 1)$ code. Let us see first how to extend the code whose parity matrix is H into a (15, 11) code. A generalization to higher dimensions will then be obvious. As we have shown, detection of the location of a single error using the matrix H is extremely simple since the error syndrome is the binary representation of the location index. This is due to the fact that row i of H is the binary representation of i, for i = 1, 2, 3, 4, 5, 6, 7. The same idea can be extended to higher dimensions where the rows of the parity matrix K of a (15, 11) code consist again of binary representations of numbers arranged in increasing order:

$$
K \;=\; \begin{array}{cccc}
0 & 0 & 0 & 1 \\
0 & 0 & 1 & 0 \\
0 & 0 & 1 & 1 \\
0 & 1 & 0 & 0 \\
0 & 1 & 0 & 1 \\
0 & 1 & 1 & 0 \\
0 & 1 & 1 & 1 \\
1 & 0 & 0 & 0 \\
1 & 0 & 0 & 1 \\
1 & 0 & 1 & 0 \\
1 & 0 & 1 & 1 \\
1 & 1 & 0 & 0 \\
1 & 1 & 0 & 1 \\
1 & 1 & 1 & 0 \\
1 & 1 & 1 & 1
\end{array}
$$

As in any linear code, the code words of this code are characterized by the fact that they yield a 0 when multiplied by the parity matrix K, and only they have this property. The problem is how to construct a code word (i.e., how to calculate the four parity bits, based on the eleven information bits, and where to locate them within a code word). In view of the discussion in section 2.4.2, the location of the parity bits corresponds to the location of the rows in K having a single 1, where in our case, these locations are powers of 2. That is, the parity bits are the first, second, fourth, and eighth in a code word. The structure of a code word is therefore p0 p1 a p2 b c d p3 e f g h i j k, where p0, p1, p2, p3 are parity bits and the rest are the original informaton bits. The parity bits are calculated from the equations whose coefficients are dictated by the columns of K. (The first column means that the sum of the last eight bits of a code word should be 0, etc.) These equations are then:

(1) p3 + e + f +g + h + i + j + k = 0
(2) p2 + b + c +d + h + i + j + k = 0
(3) p1 + a + c +d + f + g + j + k = 0
(4) p0 + a + b +d + e + g + i +k = 0

2.6   The Generating Matrix of a Systematic Code

Within the context of this book we will treat only those cases where each parity bit in a code word is calculated independently, based only on the values of some information bits. Following the discussion in section 2.4.2, the rows of the parity matrix of such codes, whose location is that of a parity bit in a code word, contain a single bit of value 1.

Now consider the case of a systematic code, in which the parity bits are located at the beginning of a code word. For illustration purposes we treat the (9, 5) code whose code words have the structure p0 p1 p2 p3 a b c d e (a b c d e is the information vector), where the parity equations are:

$$
\begin{aligned}
\text{a)} \quad & p0 = a + b + c \\
\text{b)} \quad & p1 = a + d + e \\
\text{c)} \quad & p2 = a + b + d + e \\
\text{d)} \quad & p3 = a + c + d
\end{aligned}
$$

The parity matrix of this code is then:

$$
L = \begin{array}{cccc}
1 & 0 & 0 & 0 \\
0 & 1 & 0 & 0 \\
0 & 0 & 1 & 0 \\
0 & 0 & 0 & 1 \\
1 & 1 & 1 & 1 \\
1 & 0 & 1 & 0 \\
1 & 0 & 0 & 1 \\
0 & 1 & 1 & 1 \\
0 & 1 & 1 & 0
\end{array}
$$

Note that (p0 p1 p2 p3 a b c d e)·L = 0, where the columns of L consist of the coefficients of the parity equations (a), (b), (c), (d).

Here again we observe that the rows of the parity matrix L, whose location is that of a parity bit in a code word, have a single element of value 1. More than that, the first four rows of L have the structure of a diagonal of 1 elements, with the rest of the elements being 0. This structure is a **unit matrix of dimension 4 x 4**. Generally, a (n, k) systematic code, in which the n − k parity bits appear at the beginning of a code word, has a parity matrix whose top is a unit matrix of dimension (n − k) x (n − k). (To be more accurate, each of the first n-k rows of such a code has a single 1. We can always reorder the columns of the matrix such that the 1's will appear in a diagonal structure.)

There is another matrix, beside the parity matrix, which uniquely characterizes a specific (n, k) linear code. This matrix, known as the **generating matrix** of the code, and denoted here by G, has the property that it generates the code word corresponding to an information vector I, by performing the operation I·G (i.e., multiplying I by G).

To see how a matrix G is constructed, observe the following

fundamental property of a linear code. Let C(i), C(j), C(i, j) denote, respectively, the code words corresponding to the information vectors I(i), I(j), I(i, j) where I(i) has only a single 1, in place i; I(j) has only a single 1, in place j; I(i, j) has only two 1's, in places i and j. Then C(i, j) = C(i) + C(j). For the (9, 5) code described above, we have, for example, I(1) = (1000); I(2) = (0100); I(1, 2) = (1100), and C(1) = (111110000); C(2) = (101001000); C(1, 2) = (010111000). Generally, if {p, q, r,... } is the set of the location indexes of the 1 elements in any information vector I, then the code word C corresponding to I is C(p) + C(q) + C(r) . . .. The way in which C was constructed defines our generating matrix G. For an (n, k) code, G has k rows of length n, where row i is C(i), i = 1, 2, . . ., k. The code word C is generated from the information vector I by the operation I·G, since this operation means summing those rows of G whose location is that of 1 elements in I, which is exactly the operation C(p) + C(q) + C(r) . . . described above.

Example For the (9, 5) code treated in this section, we have:

$$
G = \begin{matrix}
111110000 \\
101001000 \\
100100100 \\
011100010 \\
011000001
\end{matrix}
$$

The rows of G, starting from the top, are: C(1), C(2),...,C(5). The code word corresponding, for example, to I = (11011) is I·G = (010011011). Using our notations: I = I(1) + I(2) + I(4) + I(5), and I·G = C(1) + C(2) + C(4) + C(5).

The preceding generating matrix can be split into two parts:

$$
\begin{array}{ll}
1111 & 10000 \\
1010 & 01000 \\
1001 & 00100 \\
0111 & 00010 \\
0110 & 00001
\end{array}
$$

The right part is a 5 x 5 unit matrix. Generally, the fact that a code is systematic (having the parity bits at the beginning of a code word) is equivalent to the fact that it has a k x k unit matrix to the right of its generating matrix. (The second fact means that the code word $C = I \cdot G$, corresponding to an information vector I, ends with I, which is repeating the first fact in different words.)

The next issue that we consider, which forms the basis for some major considerations in the following chapter, is the connection between the parity matrix and the generating matrix of any systematic code (having the parity bits at the beginning of a code word). This connection is: *The part of the parity matrix below the unit matrix, equals the part of the generating matrix to the left of the unit matrix.* In our (9, 5) code this part has the form:

$$
X = \begin{array}{l}
1\ 1\ 1\ 1 \\
1\ 0\ 1\ 0 \\
1\ 0\ 0\ 1 \\
0\ 1\ 1\ 1 \\
0\ 1\ 1\ 0
\end{array}
$$

The nature of this connection is best explained by considering again our (9, 5) code. Recall that the structure of a code word is p0 p1 p2 p3 a b c d e, satisfying the parity equations:

a)   p0 = a + b + c
b)   p1 = a + d + e
c)   p2 = a + b + d + e
d)   p3 = a + c + d

Denote by **T** the fifth row of the parity matrix L, and denote by **U** the first four bits of the first line of the generating matrix G. We now show the reasoning behind the fact that **T** = **U**. Since the columns of L represent the coefficients of the parity equations, the bits of **T** represent those parity equations in which the information bit "a" appears. ("a" is the fifth bit in a code word.) The four 1's in this row represent the fact that "a" appears in all four equations. (The sixth row in L, which is 1010, represents the fact that the next information bit "b" appears in the first and third equations.)   Let us now inspect the generating matrix G. Its first row is the code word corresponding to the information vector having the bit "a" equal to 1, where the rest of the information bits are 0. When the parity bits that should be attached to such an information vector are calculated (in order to form a code word), the right hand side of any parity equation is 1 if "a" appears there, and 0 otherwise. Since in our case "a" appears in all four equations, all the four parity bits are 1. The first four bits of the first row of G, which form the vector **U**, are these parity bits, explaining why **T** = **U**. To summarize, **T** = **U** since both vectors have a 1 in place i if and only if the information bit "a" appears in parity equation i.

The equality between the sixth row of L and the first four bits in the second row of G can be demonstrated in the same way, showing why both matrices have the common submatrix X.

2.7   Review of the Concepts Introduced

Linear code: A code in which the sum of two code words is also a code word.

Hamming weight of a binary vector: The number of elements of value 1 in the vector.

Hamming distance between two binary vectors: The number of places in which the vectors differ.

Minimum Hamming distance of a code: The minimum of the distances between all possible pairs of code words in a code.

Minimum Hamming weight of a code: The minimum of the weights of all the code words in a code, excluding the "all 0" vector.

Error detection capability of a code: The maximum number of errors that can occur in a code word and that will always result in a vector that is not a code word.

Error correction capability of a code: The maximum number of errors that can occur in a code word and that always enable recovering the original code word from the erroneous vector.

Hamming code: A $(2^n, 2^n - n - 1)$ code with a minimum Hamming distance of 3.

Basic formulas: For D(min) denoting the minimum Hamming distance
of a code:

> The error detection capability of the code is D(min) − 1.

> The error correction capability of the code is
> [(D(min) − 1)/2], where [x] denotes the integer part of x.

The parity matrix of a linear code: The matrix whose columns
represent the coefficients of the parity equations that the code words of a
linear code should satisfy.

Error syndrome: The result obtained from multiplying a received
message (whose transmitted version was a code word) by the parity
matrix of the code.

Encoding: The process performed at the transmitter, where parity bits are
calculated and attached to an information vector, thus forming the
transmitted code word.

Decoding: The process performed at the receiver, where the error
syndrome is first calculated from the received message, and based on
it, error detection/correction is performed.

The generating matrix of a linear code: A matrix that generates a code
word out of an information vector, by multiplying the information vector
by this matrix.

CHAPTER 3
BASIC CIRCUITRY

3.1 Automatic Generation of the Rows of the Parity Matrix

We know that a parity matrix characterizes a code in the sense that all the code words multiplied by this matrix yield a 0 syndrome, and no other vector besides a code word has this property. It was also shown that a vector-matrix multiplication means that we sum the rows of the matrix whose location corresponds to that of the 1 elements in the vector. If we interchange, for example, rows 2 and 4 in the parity matrix and interchange also elements 2 and 4 in every code word corresponding to the same code, the multiplication of a modified code word by the modified matrix will still yield 0 since we still sum the same rows as before. Generally, if the rows of a parity matrix are scrambled randomly, with the same scrambling being applied to the elements of each code word, then the new code (whose code words are the scrambled ones) has the scrambled matrix as its parity matrix.

We next consider a way of obtaining a specific Hamming code by applying the described scrambling process on the Hamming code of Table 2.2. For abcd being the original information bits, the structure of a code word there is p0 p1 a p2 b c d. Scramble now each code word. The new order is p2 p1 p0 c a d b. The parity matrix H' of our new code, listed next, was obtained by applying the same scrambling on the rows of H.

$$
H' = \begin{array}{ccc}
1 & 0 & 0 \\
0 & 1 & 0 \\
0 & 0 & 1 \\
1 & 1 & 0 \\
0 & 1 & 1 \\
1 & 1 & 1 \\
1 & 0 & 1
\end{array}
$$

Our new Hamming code is systematic, where the parity bits are all grouped at the beginning of a code word. This is observed in the structure of H', which has a unit matrix at its top. Based on the discussion at the end of the preceding chapter, our code has a generating matrix, denoted here by G', constructed by taking the lower part of H' (the part below the unit matrix) and attaching to it a unit matrix. We then have:

$$G' = \begin{matrix} 1 & 1 & 0 & 1 & 0 & 0 & 0 \\ 0 & 1 & 1 & 0 & 1 & 0 & 0 \\ 1 & 1 & 1 & 0 & 0 & 1 & 0 \\ 1 & 0 & 1 & 0 & 0 & 0 & 1 \end{matrix}$$

A systematic code has a major practical advantage over a nonsystematic code when we consider the technical difficulty in attaching parity bits to the information bits, thereby generating a code word from the information vector. This argument is clarified when comparing the structure of a code word in a code whose parity matrix is H, and a code whose parity matrix is H'. These structures are: p0 p1 a p2 b c d   and   p2 p1 p0 c a d b.

Note that in order to construct the first code word, it is necessary to insert p2 between two information bits. The hardware necessary to implement such a task is inconvenient and expensive due to the fact that for practical purposes, the information bits are stored continuously in a register. However, in the second case the parity bits are attached to the information bits, so there is no need to split them.

Being systematic is not the only positive feature of the code whose parity matrix is H'. The other feature of this code, which is the main reason for its popularity, is the fact that both the encoding process (i.e., the generation of a code word out of an information vector) and the decoding process (i.e., the generation of the error syndrome out of a received message and correcting the errors based on the syndrome) are done very simply and elegantly using some special hardware. This feature is explained next in detail. However, before starting, some clarifications should be made. In a linear code the generation of a code word out of an information vector I is always equivalent mathematically to the multiplication of I by some generating matrix G, no matter if the code word is practically generated by a sophisticated hardware, and G is not observed explicitly. The same applies to the decoding process where the generation of the syndrome out a received message is equivalent to multiplication by a parity matrix, even if this matrix is not observed explicitly. Also, if there is any error correction process under which it is possible to correct up to t errors within a block, then the minimum Hamming distance of the code is not less than $2t + 1$, even if it may appear that the errors are corrected by some technical process that does not involve at all Hamming distance considerations. The idea behind the circuitry presented here is to facilitate the generation of code words by the transmitter, and to make it easy for the receiver to recognize whether a received message is a code word.

We show now how to generate automatically the rows of H'. This means that it will not be necessary to store this matrix as a part of the decoder (in order to multiply a received message by this matrix, thereby generating the error syndrome). Also, due to the direct link between the structures of H' and the generating matrix G', automatic generation of the rows of H' will also assist in the encoding process (where the

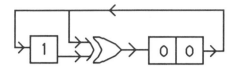

Fig. 3.1   Automatic generation of the rows of H'

information vector is multiplied by G'). A circuit that generates automatically the rows of H' is depicted in Fig. 3.1.

Fig. 3.1 depicts a three-stage feedback shift register (which shifts to the right). To clarify its operation, let us see what happens if we shift it, starting with the initial state 100. During the first shift the 1 is shifted to the second stage (we count from the left) and XORed with the 0 fed back from the right (last) stage. This 0 is also fed to the first stage. The contents of the last stage is 0, which was previously the contents of the second stage. The new contents is then 010. Further shifts yield the contents 001, and then 110, 011, 111, 101. A further shift will yield 100, which is the initial contents. The reader is urged to verify that he understands how the listed contents are obtained. The generated contents are listed below, in order:

        1 0 0
        0 1 0
        0 0 1
        1 1 0
        0 1 1
        1 1 1
        1 0 1

As clearly seen, the successive contents of the circuit of Fig. 3.1 are the rows of H'.

It should be clarified that when generating the parity matrix of a code, the length of the generating register equals the number of parity equations of the code (since the length of the register is the length of a row in the matrix, which is also the number of columns, where each column represents a parity equation).

Definition A circuit having feedback connections that are manipulated only by XOR gates is called a **"linear feedback shift register."**

The linearity of such a circuit is based on the following obvious fact: Let S1, S2, S3, . . ., be the states obtained by successive shifts of the register, starting with the initial state S0. Let T1, T2, T3, . . ., be the states obtained by successive shifts of the register, starting with the initial state T0. Then S1+T1, S2+T2, S3+T3 are the states obtained by successive shifts of the register, starting with the initial state S0+T0.

Notation A commonly used abbreviation for the concept "linear feedback shift register" is **LFSR**.

3.2 Multiplying a Message by the Parity Matrix

The multiplication of a vector (abcdefg) by the parity matrix H' is shown next:

$$
(abcdefg) \cdot
\begin{array}{ccc}
1 & 0 & 0 \\
0 & 1 & 0 \\
0 & 0 & 1 \\
1 & 1 & 0 \\
0 & 1 & 1 \\
1 & 1 & 1 \\
1 & 0 & 1 \\
\end{array}
= (a{+}d{+}f{+}g,\ b{+}d{+}e{+}f,\ c{+}e{+}f{+}g)
$$

We now show how to implement automatically the above multiplication. Fig. 3.2 depicts how the vector (a b c d e f g) is multiplied by H'. The vector is stored in a shift register and is shifted into R1 whose basic structure is that of Fig. 3.1 and whose initial contents is 000. Let us write now the contents of R1 during seven consecutive shifts of the entire circuit:

	g	0
0		
f	g	0
e	f	g
g + d	e + g	f
f + c	f + g + d	e + g
b + e + g	e + g + f + c	f + g + d
a + f + g + d	f + g + d + b + e + g	e + g + f + c

The expression for the final contents of the middle stage out of the three was shown above to be f + g + d + b + e + g. Note that g appears twice. Since + means XOR and we know that XORing a bit with itself yields 0 regardless of the value of the bit, it follows that g + g = 0, and f + g + d + b + e + g = f + d + b + e. The final contents of R1 are then: a + f + g + d, f + d + b + e, e + g + f + c, which is exactly the result of the multiplication shown before. In other words, in shifting the circuit

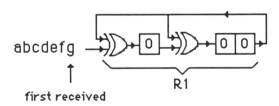

Fig. 3.2 Multiplying a vector by H'

of Fig. 3.2 seven times, we actually multiply the vector (abcdefg) by H',
where the result of this product is the contents of the LFSR. If
(abcdefg) is a received message, whose transmitted version was a
code word, the content of these stages is then the error syndrome. The
generation of the error syndrome by the decoder was thus performed
automatically without the necessity of storing H'.

We shall now look more closely at the process described above and
see what features of the circuit of Fig. 3.2 enable the multiplication
operation. First, take the case where the vector (0000001) is multiplied
by H'. We denote this vector by V7. (The 7 stands for the location of the
1 element in the vector, where the counting starts from the left.)
Mutiplying this vector by H' yields the last row of the matrix (i.e.,
$V7 \cdot H' = (101)$). Let us see why the same result is obtained by shifting
V7 into the circuit of Fig. 3.2. On the first shift, the 1 on the right of V7
is shifted into the LFSR. During the next six shifts (when the rest of V7
is shifted in), the values of the bits fed into the LFSR are all 0. In other
words, from the second shift to the seventh shift, the LFSR acts like the
generator of Fig. 3.1, starting with the initial state (100). Its final
contents is then (101), which is the last row of H'. We previously
explained how shifting V7 into the circuit of Fig. 3.2 actually performs
the operation $V7 \cdot H'$. Take now the case where the vector (1000000),
denoted by V1, is multiplied by H'. We have that $V1 \cdot H' = (100)$. This
same result is obtained by shifting V1 into the circuit of Fig. 3.2. In
order to see why this is so, observe that when the first six 0's of V1 are
shifted in, the LFSR will still contain 0. In the last shift, the 1 on the left
of V1 is shifted in, yielding (100) as the final contents of the register.

Generally, let Vi denote a vector of seven bits, having only a single element of value 1 in place i. We claim that if Vi is shifted into the circuit of Fig. 3.2, the final contents of the LFSR will be row i of H', which is exactly the result of the operation Vi·H'. This claim is proved by observing that after shifting in the first $7 - i$ 0's on the right of Vi, the LFSR will still contain 0. The 1 is then shifted in, and the circuit is shifted $i - 1$ additional times; the circuit behaves then as the generator of Fig. 3.1, yielding the i-th row of H' as the final contents of the LFSR.

Let us now see what happens when a *general* vector V, of length 7, is shifted into the circuit of Fig. 3.2. Such a V has 1 elements in places i, j, k, etc. It then consists of the sum of vectors Vi, Vj, Vk, etc. Because our system is linear, the final contents of the LFSR, after V is shifted in, equals the result obtained by shifting in separately Vi, Vj, Vk, etc., and adding these separate results. However, these separate results are the i-th, the j-th, and the k-th row of H'. Their sum then equals, by definition, the result obtained from the operation V·H'. We have thus proved generally that the circuit of Fig. 3.2 performs a vector-matrix multiplication.

3.3 The Encoding Process

In the preceding section we have demonstrated how to calculate automatically the error syndrome, based on some special properties of H'. In this section we will show how to generate automatically a code word out of an information vector. This process is the encoding process. We have already said that our code is systematic, meaning that the parity bits are attached as a continuous group to the

information vector. The parity equations presented by the columns of H'
are:

(1)   p0 + a + c + d = 0
(2)   p1 + a + b + c = 0
(3)   p2 + b + c + d = 0

Fig. 3.3 depicts how the parity bits are calculated automatically,
given the information bits.

The bits abcd which constitute the information vector are fed into an
LFSR similar to that of Fig. 3.1. Let us shift the circuit of Fig. 3.3 four
times and write the contents of the LFSR after each shift:

d	d	0
c	d+c	d
b+d	b+d+c	d+c
a+d+c	a+d+c+b+d	b+d+c

Note that a+d+c+b+d = a+b+c since the two d's cancel each other.
The final contents of R1 are then: a+d+c, a+b+c, b+d+c.

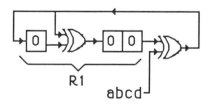

R1

abcd

Fig. 3.3 The encoder of the code whose parity matrix is H'

These are actually the values of p0, p1, p2 as dictated by equations (1), (2), (3).

We have thus demonstrated that the circuit of Fig. 3.3 automatically generates the parity bits. After they are generated, we simply have to attach them as a tail to the information bits, forming the code word p0 p1 p2 a b c d. The above discussion was merely a demonstration, and not a proof. We did not give any basic reasoning, explaining how were we able to design such a circuit. To see why the circuit of Fig. 3.3 generates the parity bits corresponding to an information vector, we list again the generating matrix of the code:

$$G = \left[\begin{array}{cc} \begin{bmatrix} 1\ 1\ 0 \\ 0\ 1\ 1 \\ 1\ 1\ 1 \\ 1\ 0\ 1 \end{bmatrix} & \begin{bmatrix} 1 & & 0 \\ & \ddots & \\ 0 & & 1 \end{bmatrix} \end{array} \right]$$

$$\underbrace{}_{X} \quad \underbrace{}_{\substack{\text{unit} \\ \text{matrix}}}$$

The parity bits attached to an information vector I form the vector I·X, where the multiplication of I by the unit-matrix part of G is equivalent to the practical situation in which I is transmitted directly as part of the information vector. We now show why the circuit of Fig. 3.3 implements the operation I·X, where I=(a, b, c, d). The rows of the submatrix X are the four successive contents of the generator depicted Fig.3.1, starting with (110). Note that the LFSR of Fig. 3.3 is the same generator. Let us see what happens when the information vector $I=(A_0, 0, 0, 0)$ is shifted into the circuit of Fig. 3.3, where A_0 can be a 0 or 1 (but the rest of the bits of I are 0 for sure). As long as A_0 is not shifted in, the LFSR still contains 0. When A_0 is shifted in, and this happens in the last shift, the contents of the LFSR is $A_0 \cdot (110)$. (If $A_0 = 1$, this 1 is shifted into the left two stages of the register, forming the contents (110). If $A_0 = 0$, the register will still contain only 0's.) Note that (110) is the first row of X, meaning that the parity bits attached to the information vector $I=(A_0, 0, 0, 0)$ are $I \cdot X$.

Generally, let I be an information vector having A_i in place i, counting from the left, where the first place is #0. (The rest of the elements of I beside A_i are 0.) When shifting I into the circuit of Fig. 3.3, the LFSR will shift $4 - i - 1$ times, containing 0. During the next shift, the element A_i is fed in, yielding the contents $A_i \cdot (110)$. The LFSR continues to run now like the generator of Fig. 3.1, for i shifts (since 0's continue to be fed in). Its final contents will be row i of X if $A_i = 1$, and "all 0" if $A_i = 0$, i.e., here we have that the parity bits attached to the information vector I are $I \cdot X$. Based on the linearity of the register, we then have that the parity bits attached to a general information vector $I=(A_0, A_1, A_2, A_3)$ form the vector $I \cdot X$. Although our proof considered specifically a (7, 4) code, it was general enough for including the case of codes of any dimension.

We can now conclude that *both the encoder and decoder use an LFSR of the same structure.* In the decoder the received message is fed into the first (left) stage of the register, where the final contents of the register form the error syndrome, as depicted in Fig. 3.2. In the encoder the information vector is fed into the last (right) stage of the register, where the final contents of the register form the parity bits attached to this vector, as depicted in Fig. 3.3.

Definition The LFSR used in both the encoder and decoder of a code is called **the generating LFSR of the code.**

3.4 Encoding/Decoding of Long and Short Vectors

Consider now the cases where we shift into the LFSR of Fig. 3.3 information vectors that are shorter or longer than 4, and then attach the contents of the LFSR to the information vector. We still get a code word whose decoder is the circuit of Fig. 3.2 (i.e., shifting the vector generated by the encoder into the circuit of Fig. 3.2 will still yield "all 0" as a final contents). Figs. 3.3 and 3.2 are then an encoder-decoder pair for any length of information vectors. The basis of this observation is that the discussions in the preceding section, and here, did not relate at all to the fact that the information vector was specifically of length 4. If it is of length 3, the parity matrix P and the generating matrix G of the code will be:

$$
P = \begin{matrix} 1\,0\,0 \\ 0\,1\,0 \\ 0\,0\,1 \\ 1\,1\,0 \\ 0\,1\,1 \\ 1\,1\,1 \end{matrix}
\qquad
G = \begin{matrix} 1\,1\,0\,1\,0\,0 \\ 0\,1\,1\,0\,1\,0 \\ 1\,1\,1\,0\,0\,1 \end{matrix}
$$

Take now the case where the information vector I = (a, b, c, d, e) of length 5 is shifted into the encoding circuit of Fig. 3.3. From the explanation given in section 3.3, we know that the final contents of register R1 will be a·(110) + b·(011) + c·(111) + d·(101) + (the contribution of e). If e=0, its contribution is (000). If e=1, the contents of R1 after the first shift is (110). It is then shifted four more times. The contribution of e to the final contents of R1 then equals the final contents of the free running generator of Fig. 3.1, after being shifted four times, starting with the initial contents (110). This final contents is (100). The parity bits generated by the encoder are then (a, b, c, d, e) · G, where G is the following generating matrix:

$$G = \begin{matrix} 1 & 1 & 0 & 1 & 0 & 0 & 0 & 0 \\ 0 & 1 & 1 & 0 & 1 & 0 & 0 & 0 \\ 1 & 1 & 1 & 0 & 0 & 1 & 0 & 0 \\ 1 & 0 & 1 & 0 & 0 & 0 & 1 & 0 \\ 1 & 0 & 0 & 0 & 0 & 0 & 0 & 1 \end{matrix}$$

Based on the connection between the parity and generating matrices of a systematic code, we have that the parity matrix P of our code is:

$$P = \begin{matrix} 1 & 0 & 0 \\ 0 & 1 & 0 \\ 0 & 0 & 1 \\ 1 & 1 & 0 \\ 0 & 1 & 1 \\ 1 & 1 & 1 \\ 1 & 0 & 1 \\ 1 & 0 & 0 \end{matrix}$$

The first and last row of P are both (100). This means that our (8, 4) code cannot correct a single error, since the occurrence of a single error in either the first or last place in a received message yields the same error syndrome. The multiplication of a message T of length 8 by the matrix P is implemented in hardware by the same decoder of Fig. 3.2. (The contents of register R1, after the message T is shifted into it, is T·P.) The explanation of this statement follows directly from the detailed discussion in section 3.2.

We now consider the possibility of making shortcuts in calculating the final contents of the register in Fig. 3.2, after very long messages are shifted into it. When shifting a message T of length 8 into it, we claimed that mathematically we perform the operation T·P. However, since the first seven rows of P consist of H', where the last row of P equals the first row of P, it follows that (a, b, c, d,e ,f, g, h) · P = (a+h, b, c, d, e, f, g) · H'. Instead of shifting into the decoder circuit a message of length 8, we can then actually shift a message of length 7, if we make a trivial precalculation (adding a to h). Generally, suppose that we want to shift the message T = (abcdefghijklmnopqrstuvwxyz) into the decoder of Fig. 3.2. We can split T into four vectors of length 7 as shown below (note that two 0's had to be attached to the message in order to have vectors of length 7):

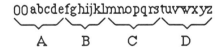

If U = A + B + C + D, then shifting T into the decoder (which will need 26 clock periods), or shifting U (which will need 7 shifts), yields the same result.

3.5   Automatic Single Error Correction

Automatic generation of the error syndrome of a received message was demonstrated in Fig. 3.2. We have not yet shown how to correct an error (i.e., how to recover the location of the error, assuming that we have only a single error), knowing the syndrome. Fig. 3.4 depicts a complete decoder that performs actual error correction.

The input to the circuit is the seven bits tuvwxyz which are the received message. After shifting the circuit seven times, starting with the depicted initial conditions, the contents of R1 are tuvwxyz. Register R2 contains the error syndrome, as discussed in detail in section 3.1. Suppose, for example, that the error is in place 5 in the received message, i.e., bit x is erroneous. (We assume the existence of not more than a single error.) Multiplying the received message by H',

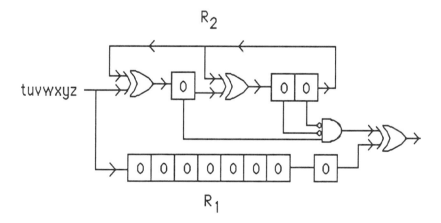

Fig. 3.4 A complete decoder

which is the parity matrix of the code to which the transmitted code word belongs, yields then as an error syndrome the fifth row of H' which is 011. Since we have shown that shifting the received message into R2 is equivalent to multiplying the message by H', we find here that the final contents of R2 is 011. Let us continue to shift the entire circuit of Fig. 3.4, after R1 already contains the received message, and R2 contains 011. Since the inputs to R2 are now successive 0's, it runs like the circuit of Fig. 3.1 (i.e., it successively generates the rows of H', starting with 011). At the same time the received message is shifted out of R1. Let us write the successive contents of R1 and R2, starting with the state where the received message resides in R1:

R1	R2
t u v w x y z	011
t u v w x y	111
t u v w x	101
t u v w	100

Note now that the erroneous bit x is fed out of R1, and resides in the isolated stage to its right, exactly when the contents of R2 are 100. This is the only state of R2 during which the output from the AND gate (there is only one such gate in Fig. 3.4) is 1. This is XORed with x on its way to the output, thus inverting its value. Since x was an erroneous bit, this inversion of x corrects the received message. (The other bits of the received message are unchanged on their way out since they are XORed with 0's.)

We have demonstrated above how a received message, having a

single error in place 5, is corrected automatically. The reader can easily see that the circuit corrects a single error located in any other place in the message. Whenever the erroneous bit is fed out of R1, it will always be XORed with a 1. All the other bits of the received message exit unchanged .

The validity of the error correction procedure can be explained as follows. Let the message tuvwxyz contain an error in place i, counting from the left. After the message is fed into the circuit of Fig. 3.4, register R2 contains the i-th row of H'. Shifting R2 further will generate rows i + 1, i + 2, etc., since R2 works now like the generator of Fig. 3.1. After 8 − i shifts the contents of R2 will be 100 (the row generated after the 7-th is the first row again). The AND gate generates now a 1. Register R1 is shifted simultaneously with R2. After 8 − i shifts, the erroneous bit resides in the isolated stage to the right of R1, and is XORed with the 1 generated by the AND gate, thus being corrected.

If the received message contains no errors, the message shifted out of the circuit of Fig. 3.4 equals the input message, after undergoing the described process. This is clarified by observing that if the received message contains no errors (i.e., it equals a code word), the contents of R2, after the message is shifted into it, is all 0. During repeated shifting of the circuit, the contents of R2 remain 0, ensuring that the output from the AND gate will never be 1, which in turn ensures that the contents of R1 are shifted out unchanged.

3.6 A General Single Error Correcting Code

The discussion in the preceding sections treated specifically a certain $(7, 4)$ code. All its circuitry consisted of variations on the LFSR of Fig. 3.1. This basic circuit has the property that when starting with any initial contents except "all 0", the circuit returns to the same initial contents only after seven shifts. This circuit has therefore a maximum periodicity in the sense that it passes through all possible states, besides all 0, before returning to the starting position. Since a parity matrix of a $(7, 4)$ code has 7 different rows of length 3, it follows that only a circuit with a maximum periodicity can generate all these rows.

Let us now generalize the above idea for any $(2^n - 1, 2^n - n - 1)$ Hamming code. The parity matrix of such a code has $2^n - 1$ rows of length n. If we wish to generate all the rows of this matrix by an n-stage LFSR (the circuit of Fig. 3.1 is a 3-stage LFSR), this circuit must have, by definition, maximum periodicity. Note that not all possible feedback connections enable maximum periodicity. For example

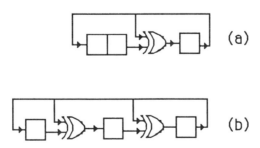 (a)

(b)

Fig. 3.5 Two linear feedback shift registers

the circuit of Fig 3.5a has maximum periodicity, like the circuit of Fig. 3.1. That of Fig. 3.5b has not, as can be verified by shifting it from any initial state. We always return to that state after less than seven shifts. This circuit cannot therefore be used as a generator of the rows of a parity matrix for a (7, 4) code since such a matrix has 7 *different* rows.

Definition The **periodicity of an LFSR related to the state S** is the minimum number of times the LFSR should be shifted, starting with S, before its contents equal S again.

Notation **Pu** denotes the periodicity of an LFSR related to the state $(1000 \ldots 0)$.

A maximum periodicity LFSR, of length n, has periodicity $2^n - 1$ in relation to any non-zero state, meaning also that for such an LFSR Pu = $2^n - 1$.

Generally, an LFSR can have different periodicities in relation to different states. Take for example the register of Fig. 3.5b. If we shift it, starting with the initial state (100), its successive contents will be (100), (010), (001), (111), (100), etc. We then have that for this LFSR Pu = 4. If we shift this register, starting with the initial state (110), its successive contents will be (110), (011), (110), etc. Here we have periodicity 2. Also, *any* LFSR will have periodicity 1 in relation to the state (000), since after a single shift we get back to (000).

Since an n-stage LFSR must have a maximum periodicity in order to generate the rows of the parity matrix of a $(2^n - 1, 2^n - n - 1)$

Hamming code, and since not all feedback connections guarantee maximal periodicity, a valid question is: How can we know which feedback connections enable maximal periodicity and which not (and this without trying out various possibilities)? Fortunately, this question has already been answered and every basic textbook on error-correcting codes gives us lists of possible feedback connections that enable maximum periodicity for various values of n. Fig. 3.6 gives two circuits having maximum periodicity (for n=4, n = 5).

There are several different LFSR's of the same length that all have maximum periodicity. For example, for n=3 the circuits of Fig. 3.1 and of Fig. 3.5a both have maximum periodicity. Any of these circuits can be used for generating the rows of the parity matrix of a Hamming code.

After selecting a generator that generates the rows of the parity matrix, a complete encoder and decoder is constructed in the same way that the circuits of Figs. 3.3 and 3.4 were constructed based on that of Fig. 3.1.

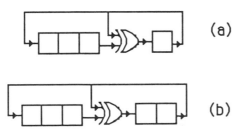

Fig. 3.6 Two LFSR's having maximum periodicity

Fig. 3.7 depicts the encoder and decoder of a (31, 26) code, based on the circuit of Fig. 3.6b.

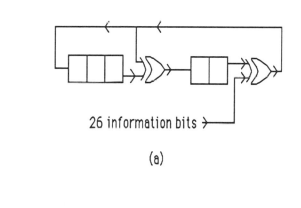

26 information bits

(a)

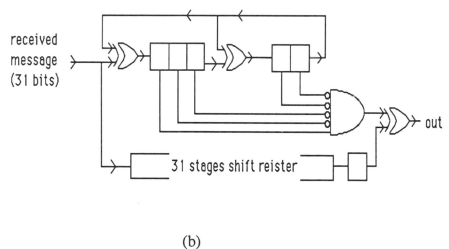

(b)

Fig. 3.7 Implementation of a (31, 26) Hamming code:
(a) encoding; (b) decoding

It is important to note that *any* LFSR can form the encoder and decoder of a linear code. (The error detection/correction capability of the code will then be an issue to be considered.) For example, the LFSR of Fig. 3.5b (which was shown not to have maximum periodicity) can be connected in a way similar to that shown in Fig. 3.3, thus adding parity bits to an information vector. If the constructed code word now enters the same LFSR, in a way similar to that depicted in Fig. 3.2, the final contents of the register will be all 0. The proof of the validity of this claim follows the same lines as the proof of the connection between the encoder of Fig. 3.3 and the decoder of Fig. 3.2 (the connection between the parity matrix and the generating matrix of a systematic code also applies here).

An issue treated in section 3.4 concerned shortcuts in the calculation of the final contents of an LFSR, after shifting a long vector T into it. We specifically treated there the circuit of Fig. 3.2, where it was shown that by "slicing" T into subvectors of length 7, and adding up the "slices", we get a vector of length 7, such that shifting it into the register is equivalent to shifting in the entire vector T. In the general case, where the LFSR is of length n, and where its feedback connections do not necessarily correspond to maximum periodicity, the idea is similar. We do not have to shift vectors longer than Pu into a register. Longer input vectors can be divided into sections of length Pu and then processed in the way described above.

CHAPTER 4
CYCLIC CODES

4.1 Some Properties of Matrices Generated by LFSR

Definition   **Shifting a vector cyclically** to the right for k places means taking out the k elements from the right-hand end of the vector and attaching them to the left-hand end.

Example Shifting the vector (1011110) cyclically to the right for four places yields the vector (1110101).

We can similarly define a left cyclic shift. Note, however, that shifting a vector of length n cyclically to the right i places is equivalent to shifting it cyclically to the left $n - i$ places.

Let M be a matrix whose rows are generated by successive shifts of an LFSR of length q, starting with the state (1000 . . . 0). *We always assume that the number of rows in M exceeds q and is limited by Pu.* (As was defined in the preceding chapter, Pu denotes the periodicity of the LFSR, related to the specified state.) Some basic features of M are listed below:

a) The first q rows of M form a unit matrix. This feature follows directly from the fact that the first q rows of M are generated by q successive shifts of the contents (1000 . . . 0). We immediately conclude that:

Conclusion 4.1 The code C whose parity matrix is M, is systematic.

Notation R_i denotes the i-th row of the matrix M.

b) The 1 elements in $R_{(q+1)}$ indicate those stages of the generating LFSR
into which the output from the last (right) stage is fed in.

Example Observe the fourth row of the matrix H' treated before (here q
= 3). This row is (110). The two left 1's indicate that the output from the
last (right) stage of the generating LFSR is fed back into the first two
stages, as clearly seen in Fig. 4.5. Examination of that circuit can also
explain why our statement is generally valid. Re-phrasing the statement
we can say:

Conclusion 4.2   If the contents of the LFSR generating M is of the form
(a, b, c, . . ., x, y), then its contents after one more shift is (0, a, b, c, . .
., x) + y $\cdot R_{(q+1)}$.

c) Let Q be a matrix of dimension q x q, consisting of the rows of M from
R_2 to $R_{(q+1)}$. Then $R_{i+1} = R_i \cdot Q$.
Example   For the matrix H', the matrix Q is:

$$Q = \begin{matrix} 010 \\ 001 \\ 110 \end{matrix}$$

Taking for example the fifth row of H' and multiplying it by Q, we get the
sixth row: $(111) \cdot Q = (101)$.

The validity of this feature follows directly from Conclusion 4.2. (It is actually a re-statement of Conclusion 4.2, noting that two successive contents of the generating LFSR represent two successive rows of M.)

The above-mentioned property can be generalized in a way that will enable us to express R_{i+2} in terms of R_i, since, based on this property, $R_{i+2} = R_{i+1} \cdot Q = [R_i \cdot Q] \cdot Q = R_i \cdot Q^2$. From the definition of the product of two matrices, the first row of Q^2 equals $Q_1 \cdot Q$ where Q_1 denotes the first row of Q. Since $Q_1 = R_2$, then by applying our property, we have that $Q_1 \cdot Q = R_3$. In other words, the first row of Q^2 is R_3. We note now that the second row of Q is R_3, and by applying the same procedure as above, we get that the second row of Q^2 is R_4. We have then proved the following conclusion.

Conclusion 4.3   Let Pj be a matrix of dimension q x q, consisting of the rows of M from R_j to $R_{(q+j-1)}$. Then $R_i \cdot Pj = R_{i+j-1}$.

Example   For the matrix H' we have:

$$
P6 = \begin{matrix} 111 \\ 101 \\ 100 \end{matrix}
$$

(We purposely took a case where we use the "end around" property of a matrix whose rows are generated by a maximum periodicity LFSR. i.e., (101) which is the last row of H' is considered to be followed by (100), which is the first row of H'.) We then have, for example, that $R_4 \cdot P6 =$ (110) $\cdot$ P6 = (010) = R_2. Note that according to Conclusion 4.3, $R_4 \cdot P6$

should equal $R_{(4+6-1)} = R_9$. However, due to the 'end around' property, R_7 is succeeded by R_1, from which it follows that $R_9 = R_2$.

d) Let G be the generating matrix of the systematic code whose parity matrix is M. Shifting any row of G, except for its last one, cyclically to the right for one place yields a code word of the code.

In order to show why the above proposition is valid, we first treat, for simplicity purposes, our (7, 4) code (which has the parity matrix H'). Observe again the structure of the generating matrix G' of our code.

$$G' = \left[\begin{bmatrix}1 1 0\\0 1 1\\1 1 1\\1 0 1\end{bmatrix}\begin{bmatrix}1 & & 0\\ & \cdot & \\ & & \cdot \\0 & & 1\end{bmatrix}\right]$$

$$\underbrace{\quad}_{X}\quad\underbrace{\quad}_{\substack{\text{unit}\\\text{matrix}}}$$

The rows of X are generated by successive shifts of the LFSR shown in Fig. 4.1.

The rows of G' are code words, corresponding to the information vectors having only a single element of value 1. Denote by Cj the j-th row of G', for j = 1, 2, 3, 4. The way by which Cj can generate the row

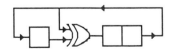

Fig. 4.1 The generator of the rows of X

C(j+1) following it, can be characterized as follows: For j=1, 2, 3, shift Cj cyclically one place to the right. This will move the 1 element in the diagonal of the unit matrix to its correct place in C(j+1). This shift will also move the contents of the register, generating the rows of X. If this shift does not move a 1 element from the X part of G' into the right part of G', then the shifted vector obtained is C(j+1), and no further action is taken. If a 1 is shifted into the right part, thereby disturbing the demand that this part should form a unit matrix, *this 1 is automatically canceled by adding the first row (C1) to the shifted Cj.* The last statement is clarified by observing the functioning of the LFSR generating the rows of X. If the cyclic shift of Cj moves a 1 into the right part of G', this means that the left three bits of Cj are of the form (a, b, 1). They form the present contents of the LFSR generating the rows of X. A further shift will move the 1 out, forming the new contents (1, a + 1, b), and the 1 shifted out is canceled. This total operation is equivalent to adding C1 to the cyclically shifted Cj.

The above discussion can be generalized to any systematic code whose parity matrix is generated by an LFSR. (This will make its generating matrix to consist of a submatrix X, of the form shown above, and a unit matrix.) Let G be the generating matrix of a code whose parity matrix is M. Any row Cj of G (beside the last one) generates the row following it by shifting Cj cyclically to the right for one place, and then either adding the first row of G to the shifted Cj or doing nothing. The validity of feature **d** is now obvious. Shifting any row of G, except its last one, cyclically to the right for one place always yields a code word. (This code word is either another row of G or the sum of another row of G and the first row. This sum is also a code word due to the linearity of the code.)

4.2   Linear Shifts of Code Words and Their Effect on the Generating Matrix

Definition   **Shifting a vector linearly** to the right by k places means taking out the k elements on the right of the vector and attaching k 0's on the left.

Example   Shifting the vector (1011110) linearly to the right by four places yields the vector (0000101).

Proposition 4.1   Let **C** be an (n, k) code whose parity matrix is M (defined in the preceding section), and let G denote the generating matrix of **C**.
1. Any code word of **C** consists of the sum of some linear shifts to the right of the first row of G, where the shifts are of no more than k − 1 places.
2. Any vector of length n that consists of the sum of some linear shifts to the right of the first row of G, where the shifts are for no more than k − 1 places, must be a code word of **C**.

Before proving the proposition, we clarify its meaning by taking, for example, our (7, 4) code, whose parity matrix is H'. Part **1** of the proposition states that any of its code words consists of the sum of some of the following vectors: (1101000), (0110100), (0011010), (0001101). This can be verified by observing the code words listed in the preceding section.   Part **2** of the proposition states that any vector of length 7, which consists of the sum of some of these four vectors, is a code word of our code.

Proof of Proposition 4.1 The proof is rather long. We decided, however, to include it all here because it presents some important general considerations. To make it more comprehensible, we divide the proof into several steps.

Step 1: **Showing the connection between cyclic shifts and linear shifts of the rows of G.**

The code **C** is systematic (Conclusion 4.1). G then has a unit matrix on its right, meaning that the rows of G, except for the last one, have a 0 as their right element. (The only 1 element in the right column of a unit matrix is in the last row.) It follows that shifting any row of G, except for its last one, *cyclically* to the right one place yields the same result as a *linear* shift one place to the right. (In the cyclic shift the 0 on the right is moved to the left. In the linear shift this 0 is dropped, and a new 0 is created on the left, yielding the same result.)

Step 2: **Expressing the rows of G in terms of linear shifts of the first row.**

In the discussion that validated property **d** it was stated that each row of G, except for the first one, is generated by shifting its preceding row *cyclically* one place to the right and sometimes adding the first row to this shift (in the case where a 1 was shifted from the X matrix part to the unit matrix part of G). From the result stated in step 1 it follows that we can replace here the word "cyclically" by the word "linearly". Since every row, from the second onward, is generated by shifting its preceding row linearly one place to the right, and sometimes adding the first row to this result, it follows that *any* row of G consists of the sum of some linear shifts to the right of the first row, where the shifts are of no more than k –

1 places. (This property definitely holds for the first row. It also holds for the second row in view of the property just stated. The third row is obtained by shifting the second row and perhaps then adding the first row. This row can then also be expressed in terms of the sum of shifts of the first row. The same holds now for the next row, etc.)

Step 3: **Dealing with a general code word.**

Any code word of the code consists of the sum of some rows of G. Since each such row consists of the sum of some linear shifts to the right of the first row, where the shifts are of no more than k-1 places, it follows that any code word also consists of the sum of some linear shifts to the right of the first row, where the shifts are of no more than k-1 places. This completes the proof of part **1** of the proposition.

Step 4: **Proving part 2 of the proposition.**

The second part of the proposition states that any vector of length n, which consists of the sum of some linear shifts to the right of the first row of G (of not more than $k - 1$ places), is a code word of **C**.

An (n, k) code has 2^k different code words. (This is the number of possible information vectors, which are each of length k. Since each information vector forms a different code word, this is also the number of code words.) Since the first part of the proposition is proved, any of these 2^k code words has the property that it consists of the sum of some linear shifts to the right of the first row of G, where the shifts are of not more than $k - 1$ places. The question is whether or not there are other vectors of length n that have the same property and that are not code words of **C**. The answer is *no*, since there are no more than 2^k vectors satisfying this property. This is because the number of possible linear shifts of a vector, where the shifts are of not more than $k - 1$ places, is exactly k. There are therefore no more than 2^k vectors of length n that can be expressed as the sum of some of these shifts. (There are 2^k different ways of summing up to k vectors, out of a set of k vectors.) All these vectors must therefore be code words of **C**.

This completes the proof of Proposition 4.1.

From Proposition 4.1 we formulate the next proposition:

Proposition 4.2 Let **C** be an (n, k) linear systematic code. Let CI denote the code word corresponding to the information vector (1000 ... 0). **C** can be generated by an LFSR if all the $k - 1$ linear right shifts of CI are also code words of the code. (The generating LFSR of a code was defined as the circuit based upon which the encoding and decoding are executed, in the form depicted in Figs. 3.2 and 3.3.)

Assuming that in our systematic code the information vector forms the right section of its corresponding code word, the validity of Proposition 4.2 is clarified by noting that CI is the code word having $k - 1$ 0's on its right, since it corresponds to the information vector (1000 ... 0). CI then forms, by definition, the first row of the generating matrix of the code. The rest of the proof of Proposition 4.2 is left as an exercise, noting that **C** is characterized by the fact that its parity matrix M is generated by an LFSR.

4.3   Properties of Maximum-Length Code Words

4.3.1 Properties of the Parity Matrix and Generating Matrix of Maximal Length Code Words

Notations

$\mathbb{H}$ denotes the set of all the matrices whose rows are generated by successive shifts of an LFSR, where the LFSR starts shifting with the initial state $(1000\ldots0)$ and stops shifting one step before getting back to the initial state (i.e., the number of rows in a matrix belonging to $\mathbb{H}$ is Pu; or, if the last row of any matrix in the set $\mathbb{H}$ forms the contents of its generating LFSR, and the LFSR is shifted once more, its new contents will be $(1000\ldots0)$).

$\mathbb{C}$ denotes the set of all the codes having a parity matrix in $\mathbb{H}$. The length of a code word in a code belonging to $\mathbb{C}$ is then the value of Pu of the corresponding generating LFSR. Such code words are defined as **maximum-length code words**.

Features **a** through **d** listed in section 4.1 are also valid, of course, for any matrix belonging to $\mathbb{H}$.   Conclusion 4.1 means that any code belonging to $\mathbb{C}$ is systematic. The following statements relate only to matrices belonging to the set $\mathbb{H}$:

e) Let R_n denote the last row of a matrix M belonging to $\mathbb{H}$. Shifting R_n cyclically one place to the right yields $R_{(q+1)}$.

This is demonstrated by again observing the matrix H' (which belongs to $\mathbb{H}$). Its R_n is (101). Shifting it cyclically one place to the right yields (110), which is its $R_{(q+1)}$. We now prove that this statement is valid for any matrix M in $\mathbb{H}$. Note that if R_n forms the contents of the generating LFSR, then its contents after one more shift is (1000 ... 0). (This is based on the definition of $\mathbb{H}$.) The 1 on the left of this new contents can be there only if the preceding contents R_n had a 1 on the right (this 1 was then shifted into the left place), and the structure of R_n is then (a, b, c, . . ., x, 1). Based on Conclusion 4. 2 we then have that $(1000...0) = (0,a,b,c,...,x) + R_{(q+1)}$. It follows that $R_{(q+1)} = (0,a,b,c,...,x) + (1000...0) = (1,a,b,c,...,x)$. Since the expression $(1,a,b,c,...,x)$ is for a cyclic shift of R_n, one place to the right, we have proved our statement generally.

f) Let the matrix M, belonging to the set $\mathbb{H}$, be the parity matrix of a code. (This code then belongs to $\mathbb{C}$ and is systematic in view of conclusion 4.1.) Let G be the generating matrix of that code. Then shifting the last row of G cyclically one place to the right, yields the first row of G.

Before proving this property, let us demonstrate it for the code whose parity matrix is H'. Its generating matrix is:

$$
G' = \begin{array}{ccccccc}
1 & 1 & 0 & 1 & 0 & 0 & 0 \\
0 & 1 & 1 & 0 & 1 & 0 & 0 \\
1 & 1 & 1 & 0 & 0 & 1 & 0 \\
1 & 0 & 1 & 0 & 0 & 0 & 1
\end{array}
$$

Shifting the last row of G' cyclically one place to the right yields its first row. In order to understand why this is generally true, note again the following basic structure of the generating matrix G:

$$
G = \begin{bmatrix} \begin{bmatrix} \\ \\ \\ \end{bmatrix} & \begin{bmatrix} 1 & & 0 \\ & \cdot & \\ & \cdot & \\ 0 & & 1 \end{bmatrix} \\ \underbrace{}_{X} & \underbrace{}_{\substack{\text{unit} \\ \text{matrix}}} \end{bmatrix}
$$

Using the notations R_n and $R_{(q+1)}$ introduced above, we know that the matrix X consists of the rows of the parity matrix M, from $R_{(q+1)}$ to R_n. From the relation between $R_{(q+1)}$ and R_n, proved in **e** above, we have that:

$$
X = \begin{bmatrix} 1abc....x \\ \cdot \\ \cdot \\ abc....x1 \end{bmatrix}
$$

and therefore:

$$
G = \begin{bmatrix} \begin{bmatrix} 1abc....x \\ \cdot \\ \cdot \\ abc....x1 \end{bmatrix} & \begin{bmatrix} 100...0 \\ \cdot \\ \cdot \\ 000...1 \end{bmatrix} \end{bmatrix}
$$

Observing the last form of G, it is now obvious why shifting its last row cyclically one place to the right yields its first row.

4.3.2 Cyclic Shifts of Maximal Length Code Words

Definition   A code is **cyclic** if the vectors obtained by any cyclic shift of any of its code words are also code words.

Our (7, 4) code (whose parity matrix is H') is cyclic, as clearly seen from the following list of its code words:

(0000000)	(1010001)	(1110010)
(0100011)	(0110100)	(1100101)
(1000110)	(0010111)	(1101000)
(0111001)	(0011010)	(1001011)
(1011100)	(0001101)	(0101110)
(1111111)		

Proposition 4.3 **Any code belonging to $\mathbb{C}$ is cyclic.** In other words: any code generated by an LFSR, where the length of a code word is Pu, is cyclic.

This major proposition explains why the codes belonging to $\mathbb{C}$ are called **Cyclic Codes'**. Before proving the proposition we should elaborate a bit more; the concept 'Cyclic Codes' usually refers to any code generated by an LFSR, regardless of the length of a code word. However, it should be clarified that the code words of such codes do not necessarily have the cyclic property unless the length of a code word is Pu.

Proof of Proposition 4.3   As was stated, any code belonging to $\mathbb{C}$ is systematic. Let G denote the generating matrix of our code. This matrix has properties **d** and **f** above. According to **d**: shifting any row of G, except the last one, cyclically one place to the right, yields a code word. According to **f**: shifting the last row of G cyclically one place to the right yields the first row, which we know is a code word. To conclude: shifting *any* row of G cyclically one place to the right yields a code word.

Any code word C in our code consists of the sum of some rows of G. (Multiplying an information vector I by G yields the code word corresponding to I, where such a multiplication means summing some rows of G.) A cyclic shift of C one place to the right can be regarded as a shift of all the rows of G whose sum yields C. In view of what was said above, each such shifted row of G yields a code word. The sum of these code words, which is nothing but the shifted C, is therefore also a code word. We then proved that shifting any code word in our code, cyclically one place to the right, yields a code word. This proves that shifting a code word by *any* number of places also yields a code word. (If a single shift to the right yields a code word, applying a single shift consecutively several times will also yield a code word, since every result in this chain is a code word.) Proposition 4.3 has thus been proved.

4.4   The Encoder and Decoder of a Code Satisfying the Parity Equations of Several Independent Codes

4.4.1 *The Problem*

Fig. 4.2 depicts a circuit consisting of two LFSR's, denoted by R1 and R2, fed by a common input. There is a code C whose code words have the property that after being shifted into the circuit of Fig. 4.2, *both*

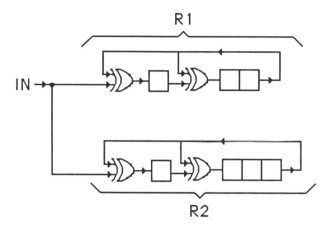

Fig. 4.2 Connecting two LFSR's in parallel

registers will have "all 0" contents. This code can be generated by a single LFSR. (A simple way of showing that such an LFSR exists is by applying Proposition 4.2.) We are next concerned with the connection between this generating LFSR and the registers R1, R2.

4.4.2 Determining the Length of the Generating LFSR

By now it should be clear that the length of the LFSR, which generates a code, equals the number of parity equations that a code word must satisfy. Since shifting a code word of our code **C** into either R1 or R2 (Fig. 4.2) yields an "all 0" syndrome, it follows that the code words of **C** must satisfy two independent sets of parity equations. These are the three equations dictated by the code whose decoder is only R1 and the four equations dictated by the code whose decoder is only R2. We can then construct the code words of **C** by satisfying seven independent parity equations. (We do not propose that there *must* be seven equations; fewer are sometimes sufficient. This will happen if the two sets of equations dictated by the two independent codes have some equations in common.

However, seven equations are certainly sufficient for representing the parity constraints of both codes, and the following discussion will be based on this number.)

Note that the (n, k) values of **C** were not determined at this stage. We only determined that n − k = 7.

4.4.3 Looking for a Vector Whose Elements Represent the Feedback Connections of the Required LFSR

We have already mentioned that the feedback connections of the LFSR that generates an (n, k) systematic code are indicated by the bits in the (q + 1)th row of the parity matrix of the code, where q = n − k. These same bits are the first q bits in the first row of the generating matrix of the code. We clarify this again by observing the first row of the generating matrix of the popular (7, 4) code used in this text, whose parity matrix is H'. This row is (1101000). The first three bits are (110), indicating that the feedback line from the right stage of the generating LFSR is fed into the two left stages, as shown in Fig. 3.1. The first row of the generating matrix of a code, which is the code word CI corresponding to the information vector (1000 ... 0), is characterized by having k − 1 0's on its right (i.e., the nonzero elements of CI are all confined to the left q + 1 places). It is worth noting that the (q+1)th bit in this row is definitely 1, since it is the 1 element of the information vector. Also, in all practical cases, the first bit in this row is 1. (One way of explaining this fact is by observing that a 1 in first place indicates that the feedback line is fed into the first stage of the generating LFSR. This must be the case since otherwise we could throw away the first stage without affecting the behavior of the circuit.)

It follows that in order to find the LFSR generating our code **C** (for which we decided that q = 7), it is sufficient to find a nonzero vector of length 8, such that after it has been shifted into R1 and R2, they both yield 'all 0' contents. Next we consider the properties of this vector in some more detail.

Feeding the vector **v1** = (11010000) into R1 yields (000) as its final contents. This can be explained in two ways. a) The vector (1101000) is the code word CI of the code generated by R1, and the extra 0 that **v1** has makes no difference; b) by inspection, shifting (1101) into R1 yields (000) because the 1 on the right is fed out of the register and enters the XOR gate exactly when the other two 1's enter the other inputs of the gates. Therefore they all cancel each other.

For reasons already discussed extensively we know that feeding a vector that consists of the sum of right linear shifts of **v1** into R1, where the shifts are of not more than four places, will also yield a (000) contents. Similarly, entering **v2** = (11001000) into R2 yields (0000) as its final contents. The same holds for a vector that consists of the sum of right linear shifts of **v2**, where the shifts are of not more than three places. We look now for a vector **v3** that *simultaneously* consists of the sum of linear shifts of **v1** and linear shifts of **v2** (where the shifts are of not more than four and three places, respectively). **v3** is then a vector of length 8, having the property that when being shifted into R1 and R2, they both yield 'all 0' contents. **v3** is thus exactly the vector we are looking for, indicating the feedback connections of the generating LFSR of our code **C**.

4.4.4 *Finding the Vector v3*

Proposition 4.4

$$v3 = (11001) \cdot \begin{matrix} 11010000 \\ 01101000 \\ 00110100 \\ 00011010 \\ 00001101 \end{matrix} = (10110101)$$

Proof Consider the following equality:

$$(vwxyz) \cdot \begin{matrix} abcd0000 \\ 0abcd000 \\ 00abcd00 \\ 000abcd0 \\ 0000abcd \end{matrix} = (abcd) \cdot \begin{matrix} vwxyz000 \\ 0vwxyz00 \\ 00vwxyz0 \\ 000vwxyz \end{matrix}$$

The equality means that multiplying a vector **a** by a matrix whose rows consist of linear shifts of a vector **b** is equivalent to multiplying **b** by a matrix whose rows consist of linear shifts of **a**.

In order to see why the equality holds, simply perform the multiplication operation on each side, and verify that the same vector is obtained as a result. (The elements of this vector are av, bv+aw, cv+bw+ax, etc.)

Specifically we can say that:

$$(11001) \cdot \begin{matrix} 11010000 \\ 01101000 \\ 00110100 \\ 00011010 \\ 00001101 \end{matrix} = (1101) \cdot \begin{matrix} 11001000 \\ 01100100 \\ 00110010 \\ 00011001 \end{matrix}$$

The rows of the two matrices in the above equation consist of linear shifts of **v1** and **v2**. According to the left-hand side of the equation, the result of the multiplication consists of the sum of some linear shifts of **v1**. According to the right-hand side of the equation, the same result consists of the sum of some linear shifts of **v2**. This result, which is the vector 10110101, then consists of the sum of some linear shifts of both **v1** and **v2**, which is exactly the definition of **v3**. This completes the proof of the proposition.

4.4.5 *Constructing the LFSR Corresponding to the Vector v3*

The vector **v3** = (10110101) gives the LFSR that generates our code **C** in the sense that its first seven bits indicate the feedback connections of the register, as depicted in Fig. 4.3.

The first seven bits of **v3** are written, in order, below the corresponding seven stages of the LFSR of Fig, 4.3a. A stage is connected to the feedback line if and only if a 1 is written below it. Figs. 4.3b and c depict how this register is used in the encoding and decoding circuitry of the code **C**.

We now generalize the process of finding the LFSR whose function is equivalent to two LFSR's connected in parallel (in the way that the LFSR of Fig.4.3 is equivalent to those of Fig. 4.2). Generally we are given a circuit of the form shown in Fig. 4.4.

We are asked to find the LFSR that replaces the two registers in the figure. The feedback connections of our LFSR will be found by multiplying a vector **v** by a matrix **M**, where **v** represents the feedback connections of one register and the rows of **M** consist of linear shifts of the vector representing the feedback connections of the other register.

This is clarified by again observing the specific vector-matrix multiplication given in Proposition 4.4.

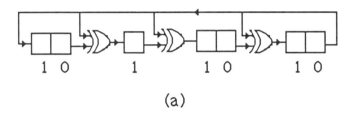

(a)

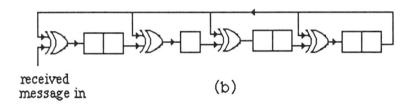

received
message in   (b)

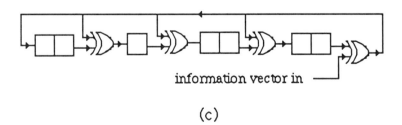

information vector in

(c)

Fig. 4.3   (a) A register whose feedback connections correspond
                  to the first seven bits of **v3**.
              (b) The syndrome generator of the code **C**.
              (c) The encoder of the code **C**.

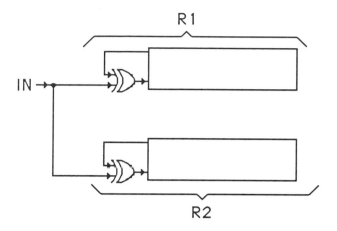

Fig. 4.4 A general case of two LFSR's connected in parallel

A major question to ask is: Are there other LFSR's that function like two given registers connected in parallel, in addition to the one found by

our specific process, and where the length of such an LFSR does not exceed the sum of the lengths of the two individual registers? The answer is, in many cases, yes. This is not the case for the specific circuit of Fig. 4.2. Such a case is demonstrated, however, in the next chapter.

4.5   Maximum-Length Sequences

4.5.1 Introduction

Introductory Note The theory of maximum length sequences presented in this section is not directly related to the theory of error- correcting codes. It is based, however, on the considerations treated up to now, and is included in the text for two reasons. a) it can serve as an elegant tool for digging deeper into the presented material;   b) it serves in many applications ranging from spread spectrum techniques and random number generation to coding theory and cryptography. This material deserves a book on its own and only some basic features are discussed here. This entire section can be skipped, however, without loss of continuity.

Definition Let a maximum periodicity LFSR of length n be shifted $2^n - 1$ times, starting with any nonzero initial contents. The sequence of bits of length $2^n - 1$, consisting of the successive contents of any stage of the LFSR (generated during the shifts) is called a **maximum-length sequence generated by an LFSR**. For brevity, we will term this sequence a **maximum-length sequence**.

Example Consider the maximum periodicity LFSR of Fig. 3.1 (redrawn as Fig. 4.1).

The sucessive contents of this LFSR, starting with the initial state (111) are (111), (101), (100), (010), (001), (110), (011). The next contents is again (111). The sucessive contents of the three stages are the following strings of length 7:
Left stage:(1110010).
Middle stage: (1001011).
Right stage: (1100101).
Any of these three sequences is a maximum length sequence.

This section deals with specific properties of maximum-length sequences.

Property 1   Any string of n successive bits in a maximum- length-sequence of length $2^n - 1$ is different. (Such a string is called **n-tuple**.) This includes the case where the bits of the sequence are considered to be ordered cyclically (i.e., the last bit is considered to be followed by the first). The only n-bit pattern, which does not exist as an n-tuple in the sequence, is the "all 0" pattern.

As an example take the sequence (1110010) of length $2^3 - 1$. Starting from the left, we see successively the following 3-tuples: (111), (110), (100), (001), (010), (101), (011).

The LFSR of Fig. 3.1 is the generator of the rows of the matrix H' treated in detail in the preceding sections. The three maximum-length sequences introduced in the preceding example are the three columns of H' shifted cyclically. (The reader is advised to compare these sequences to the columns of H'.) Although the entire subject of maximum-length sequences can be treated without connection to the parity matrices of cyclic Hamming codes, we decided to adopt such a connection here for tutorial purposes.

From now on, whenever we feel it convenient, we will refer to *the columns of the parity matrix of a cyclic Hamming code,* rather than to the concept *maximum-length sequences*, knowing that they mean the same thing. We will consider the column vectors of H' as row vectors (i.e., we write them horizontally instead of vertically).

4.5.2   *The Recursion Relation Associated with a Maximum-Length Sequence*

Observe that any element a_n in any column of H' satisfies the relation $a_n =$

$a_{n-2} + a_{n-3}$ (i.e., each element equals the sum of the two elements preceding it by two and three places, counting from the left).

For example, consider the column (1001011). The 1 in the fourth place from the left, equals the sum of the elements in the second and first place. (These are 0 and 1, respectively.) The 0 at the fifth place equals the sum of the two elements in the third and second place. (Both are 0.) This relation, known as a **recursion relation,** applies to a cyclic ordering of the elements of the vector (1001011). For example, the first element (which is considered to be preceded by the seventh element) equals the sum of the sixth and fifth elements.

The above recursion relation is explained by taking the code word V = (1101000) of the (7, 4) Hamming code whose parity matrix is H'. The fact that V is a code word means that V·H' = (000). Let us denote the three columns of H' by H'(1), H'(2), and H'(3). The operation V·H'(1) means, in practice, summing the first, second, and fourth elements of H'(1). Since V·H' = 0, it follows that the sum of these three elements of H'(1) is 0. Since our code is cyclic, it follows that (0110100)·H'(1) =0, meaning that the sum of the second, third, and fifth elements of H'(1) is also 0. By continuing this process, we see why the elements of H'(1) satisfy the recursion relation $a_n = a_{n-2} + a_{n-3}$. The same argument can now be applied for the columns H'(2) and H'(3), explaining why they also satisfy the same recursion relation.

We showed how, from the code word (1101000), we find that all the columns of H' satisfy a certain recursion relation, where the coefficients of the recursion relation are based on the nonzero elements of the code word V, that is: the relation $a_n = a_{n-2} + a_{n-3}$ corresponds to the pattern (1101) in the code word. (The elements of this pattern, *counting from right to left* correspond, respectively, to the coefficients of a_{n-3}, a_{n-2}, a_{n-1}, and a_n of the recursion relation.) Had we taken another code word, and applied the same arguments given before, we would have apparently obtained another recursion relation corresponding to the nonzero elements of this code word. However, from Proposition 4.1, it follows that this "other" relation can still be expressed in terms of our basic relation $a_n = a_{n-2} + a_{n-3}$. Note that the pattern (1101) also corresponds to the structure of the feedback connections of the LFSR generating the rows of H' (Fig. 3.1).

From the connection discussed before between maximum- length sequences and the columns of matrices, the preceding arguments can be generalized as follows:

Property 2 The elements of a maximum-length sequence satisfy the recursion relation specified by the structure of the feedback connections of the LFSR generating the sequence.

This leads us directly to the next property.

Property 3 Any n sucessive elements of a maximum-length sequence uniquely determine the rest of the elements.

The above property can be explained as follows. The recursion relation specified by the generating LFSR of the sequence shows how the value of an element is determined by the values of the n elements preceding it. In other words, given n successive elements of the sequence, the value of the element following them is determined by the recursion relation. The last n elements out of the n+1 elements that we have now, determine the next element, etc.

Since a maximum-length sequence of length $2^n - 1$ contains all possible non-zero n-tuples, it is impossible that two maximum-length sequences satisfying the same recursion relation will be different. (The only difference can be a cyclic shift.) Our logic follows. Given two such sequences, select a certain n-tuple in both. (Any n-tuple which is found in one is also found in the other since they cover all possibilities.) The elements following it are the same in both sequences since they both satisfy the same recursion relation. We then have the following property.

Property 4 All the maximum-length sequences satisfying the same recursion relation are identical. (The only difference among them can be a cyclic shift.)

Property 4 explains why the three columns of H' are cyclic shifts of the same vector.

The LFSR generating the rows of the parity matrix of a Hamming code can be considered to be a generator of maximum-length sequences. Simply load it with a nonzero initial state, and shift it $2^n - 1$ times (where the LFSR is of length n). The successive contents of any of its stages form a maximum-length sequence. For each such generator *there is, however, another circuit generating the same sequence*. This argument is

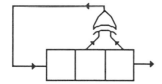

Fig. 4.5   Another generator of the maximum-length sequence
generated by the circuit of Fig. 3.1

clarified by considering the circuit depicted in Fig. 4.5 which generates
the same sequence as the one generated by the circuit of Fig. 3.1.

To understand why the circuits of Figs. 3.1 and 4.5 generate the same
maximum-length sequence, observe that in the latter any new bit entering
the LFSR from the left equals the sum of the two bits which preceded it
by 2 and 3 places. In other words, *we see explicitly how the recursion
relation $a_n = a_{n-2} + a_{n-3}$ is satisfied.* Since a maximum-length sequence is
determined uniquely by its recursion relation (Property 4), the two circuits
generate the same maximum-length sequence. Note the basic difference
between the structure of the two circuits. That of Fig. 3.1 uses "fed-in"
feedback connections. That is, the output from the last (right) stage is fed
back into some preceding stages. The circuit of Fig. 4.5 uses "fed-out"
connections, where the contents of some stages are XORed and fed into
the first (left) stage.

Property 5 A maximum-length sequence can be generated by two kinds
of LFSR, using either fed-in or fed-out connections.

Next we consider the operation of summing several cyclic shifts of the same maximum-length sequence. Observe, for example, that the sum of any subset of the three columns of H', which are cyclic shifts of the same maximum-length sequence, yields again a cyclic shift of the same sequence. (e.g. the sum of the first and third columns is (1011100). The sum of all the three columns is (1110010).)

The above is based on the self-explanatory fact that *the sum of sequences which all satisfy the same recursion relation also satisfies the same relation.* (If every element in each sequence equals the sum of two elements preceding it 2 and 3 places, the same will hold for their sum.)

Property 6 The sum of cyclic shifts of a certain maximum-length-sequence yields the same sequence (with a certain cyclic shift).

4.5.3 Why Maximum-Length Sequences Are Also Called Pseudo-Random Sequences

Explanatory Remark In this subsection we deal with multiplication and addition of numbers which are not necessarily only 0 or 1. The addition will sometimes mean ordinary addition of numbers and will sometimes mean XOR operation, as customarily done in this book. To avoid confusion, we denote an ordinary addition operation by + and an XOR operation by $\oplus$. From the next subsection on, we return to our previous convention, denoting again an XOR operation by +.

The general theory concerning the various definitions of randomness is outside the scope of this book. Here we treat one aspect of this theory.

Definition   Let V_i denote the vector obtained by shifting a vector V cyclically i places to the right. The **cyclic auto-correlation** of V is a vector of the same length whose i-th element is the scalar product $V \cdot V_i$.

Example   The cyclic auto-correlation of the vector $V = (1, 2, 3, 4, 5)$, is a vector $A(V) = (A0, A1, A2, A3, A4)$ where:

A0 – $(1,2,3,4,5) \cdot (1,2,3,4,5) = 1 \cdot 1 + 2 \cdot 2 + 3 \cdot 3 + 4 \cdot 4 + 5 \cdot 5$

$= 1 + 4 + 9 + 16 + 25 = 55$

A1 $= (1,2,3,4,5) \cdot (5,1,2,3,4) = 45$

A2 $= (1,2,3,4,5) \cdot (4,5,1,2,3) = 40$

A3 $= (1,2,3,4,5) \cdot (3,4,5,1,2) = 40$

A4 $= (1,2,3,4,5) \cdot (2,3,4,5,1) = 45$

We can describe the auto-correlation function of a vector V in terms of the vector-matrix multiplication $V \cdot M$, where the columns of M consist of ordered cyclic shifts of V.

Example   The cyclic auto-correlation of the vector (abcde) is the result of the product:

$$(abcde) \cdot \begin{matrix} aedcb \\ baedc \\ cbaed \\ dcbae \\ edcba \end{matrix}$$

Intuitively we can say that the elements of the auto-correlation function indicate the results obtained from "overlapping" the elements of a vector and cyclic ordering of these elements, and trying to look for similarities. The first element of this function is the result obtained from "overlapping" the vector on itself, giving some kind of a peak in the function. If the other values of the auto-correlation function are constantly low, this indicates a disorder among the elements of the vector, meaning "good" random properties.

Take now the specific vector V = (-1, -1, -1, +1, +1, -1, +1). The cyclic auto-correlation of V is:

$$
\begin{array}{l}
\ -1,\ \ 1,-1,\ \ 1,\ \ 1,-1,-1 \\
\ -1,-1,\ \ 1,-1,\ \ 1,\ \ 1,-1 \\
\ -1,-1,-1,\ \ 1,-1,\ \ 1,\ \ 1 \\
(-1, -1, -1,\ \ 1,\ \ 1, -1,\ \ 1) \cdot\ \ \ 1,-1,-1,-1,\ \ 1,-1,\ \ 1 \\
\ \ \ 1,\ \ 1,-1,-1,-1,\ \ 1,-1 \\
\ -1,\ \ 1,\ \ 1,-1,-1,-1,\ \ 1 \\
\ \ \ 1,-1,\ \ 1,\ \ 1,-1,-1,-1 \\
\end{array}
$$

$$= (7, -1, -1, -1, -1, -1, -1)$$

Based on the auto-correlation function of V, its elements are considered to have an optimum randomness. (Readers more familiar with the subject will recognize here a "discrete Delta function.") We show next how we have arrived at this vector V.

Let us see first a simple connection between an XOR operation and the multiplication of signed numbers. Comparing the two columns of Table 4.1 we observe an interesting similarity. An XOR operation can be "transformed" into a product operation between signed numbers with absolute value 1, by making the following substitutions:

$$\oplus \ \rightarrow \ \cdot \ \ ; 0 \rightarrow 1 \ ; \ 1 \rightarrow \ -1$$

$0 \oplus 0 = 0$	$+1 \cdot +1 = +1$
$0 \oplus 1 = 1$	$+1 \cdot -1 = -1$
$1 \oplus 0 = 1$	$-1 \cdot +1 = -1$
$1 \oplus 1 = 0$	$-1 \cdot -1 = +1$

Table 4.1   Demonstrating the similarity between a XOR operation
and the multiplication of signed numbers

Let us see how Property 6 of maximum-length sequences is transformed, using the above substitutions. On the left, below, we XOR two cyclic shifts of a maximum-length sequence, obtaining a result that is a cyclic shift of the same sequence. On the right we write the same operation using the above substitutions, denoting the obtained vectors by X, Y, and Z:

$$
\begin{array}{llll}
& 1110010 & -1, -1, -1, \ 1, \ 1, -1, \ 1 & = X \\
\oplus & \underline{1011100} & \underline{-1, \ 1, -1, -1, -1, \ 1, \ 1} & = Y \\
& 0101110 & 1, -1, \ 1, -1, -1, -1, \ 1 & = Z \\
\end{array}
$$

Note that based on the definition of scalar product between two vectors, *the sum of the elements of Z is the scalar product X·Y*. In the above demonstration this scalar product (i.e., the sum of the elements of Z) is -1. We claim now that *if X and Y were originated from different shifts of a maximum- length sequence, then their scalar product is always -1, regardless of the dimension of the maximum-length sequence*. This is explained by observing that the number of elements of value 1 and value -1 in X, Y, and Z is correspondingly the number of 0 elements and 1 elements in the original maximum-length sequence. Based on Property 1 of maximum-length sequences, it follows directly that in any such sequence of any length $2^n - 1$, the number of 1 elements exceeds by 1 the number of 0 elements. It then follows that the difference between the number of elements of value -1 and the number of elements of value 1 in Z is 1. The sum of the elements of Z (i.e., the scalar product of X and Y) is therefore -1. If the sequences X and Y (of length $2^n - 1$) are identical, then their scalar product equals $2^n - 1$, since we sum $2^n - 1$ elements of value 1. We then have the following:

Property 7 Let S denote a sequence of elements of value $\pm$ 1, obtained from a maximum-length sequence of length $2^n - 1$ by the described substitution process. Then the auto-correlation function of S has the value $2^n - 1$ at place 0, while the rest of the elements have the constant value -1.

Property 7 explains why maximum-length sequences are sometimes called **pseudo-random sequences**. The word 'random' is now clear. The word "pseudo" means that unlike pure noise, which cannot be precisely reconstructed even if the same generation process is used, precise copies of our sequence can be reconstructed if the same generating LFSR is used, starting with the same initial state.

4.5.4   *Finding the Feedback Connections of an LFSR That Generates a Maximum-Length Sequence, Out of the Sequence Itself*

Property 8 The feedback connections of an LFSR of length n that generates a maximum-length sequence, can be recovered from any given 2n successive bits of the generated sequence.

The above property is proved by first considering that the feedback connections of an LFSR that generates a maximum-length sequence correspond to the coefficients of the recursion relation that characterizes the sequence. We are then faced with the problem of finding the recursion relation. The way to find it is demonstrated by considering an example.

The sequence $S = (110101111000100)$ is a maximum-length sequence of periodicity 15 (generated by an LFSR of length 4). Every element a_n in it satisfies a recursion relation of the form: $a_n = A \cdot a_{n-1} + B \cdot a_{n-2} + C \cdot a_{n-3} + D \cdot a_{n-4}$, where A, B, C, and D are the coefficients of the recursion relation. Since the same coefficients hold for any a_n, we can find their values by constructing four independent equations, using a different a_n. (It can be simply shown that D is always 1, leaving us with three unknowns. However, here we will not make use of this, and we treat D as an unknown.)

An equation with the four unknowns (A, B, C, D) is constructed out of five consecutive bits from S. Take for example the first five bits 11010. We can index them as a_1, a_2, a_3, a_4, a_5. The general relation $a_n = A \cdot a_{n-1} + B \cdot a_{n-2} + C \cdot a_{n-3} + D \cdot a_{n-4}$ then has here the form $a_5 = A \cdot a_4 + B \cdot a_3 + C \cdot a_2 + D \cdot a_1$. Substituting the values 11010 for a_1, a_2, a_3, a_4, a_5, we get
(1) $0 = A \cdot 1 + B \cdot 0 + C \cdot 1 + D \cdot 1$

Similarly, the five consecutive bits of S, starting with the second, are 10101. They form the equation:

(2) $1 = A \cdot 0 + B \cdot 1 + C \cdot 0 + D \cdot 1$

The five consecutive bits of S, starting with the third, are 01011, forming the equation:

(3) $1 = A \cdot 1 + B \cdot 0 + C \cdot 1 + D \cdot 0$

The five consecutive bits of S, starting with the fourth, are 10111, forming the equation :

(4) $1 = A \cdot 1 + B \cdot 1 + C \cdot 0 + D \cdot 1$

The solution to the four equations is: A=0, B=0, C=1, D=1. Our recursion relation is then $a_n = a_{n-3} + a_{n-4}$, corresponding to the generating LFSR of Fig. 4.6.

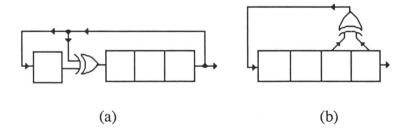

(a)   (b)

Fig. 4.6   LFSR's corresponding to the recursion $a_n = a_{n-3} + a_{n-4}$.
(a) Fed-in connections. (b) Fed-out connections.

Note that the four equations from which we recovered our generating
LFSR were obtained by taking eight consecutive bits of S, starting with
the first bit. The same purpose (i.e., constructing four equations) could
be served by taking any other eight consecutive bits of S, thus clarifying
the general case stated in Property 8. (We have not proved that the
equations obtained this way are independent. This is, however, true.)

4.5.5 Advancement Operations in Maximum-Length Sequences

Given any nonzero n-tuple T it is possible to determine all the bits
following T in a maximum-length sequence of periodicity $2^n - 1$ by
shifting the generating LFSR (with the fed-out feedback connections),
starting with the state T.

In the following example, like all the ones that will follow, we adopt a
right-to-left counting. That is, the sequence (10$\underline{1011}$) starts with the
underlined 4-tuple. Its first, second, and third bits are, respectively, 1, 1,
and 0. The reason for this convention is avoidance of confusion when
analyzing the behavior of right-shift LFSR's. As an example for the way
by which the bits following T are recovered, consider the 4-tuple T =
(1011). Like any other nonzero 4-tuple, T appears somewhere, and only
once, in the maximum-length sequence generated by the LFSR's of Fig.
4.6. In order to find the bits following T in this sequence, feed T into the
LFSR of Fig. 4.6b. Successive shifts of the register will generate the
maximum-length sequence (001000111101011). Note that the rightmost
bits are the ones that were shifted out first from the LFSR. The reason
for selecting the LFSR with the fed-out feedback connections is because

the first n bits shifted out by this register equal the initial contents T, which is not the case with the register that has fed-in connections.

We are now concerned with the following problem. Given an LFSR that generates a maximum-length sequence of periodicity $2^n - 1$, how can we modify it such that whenever it is fed with an initial n-tuple T, the output sequence will start i places after T, for any specified i.

In order to clarify the problem, take the sequence (001000111101011). It starts with the 4-tuple T = (1011). Starting from the 5-th place, the sequence is (... 00011110). The question is how to modify the circuit of Fig. 4.6b, such that, when it is fed with T, it will generate the sequence (... 00011110).

Property 9 Let **S** be a maximum-length sequence of periodicity $2^n - 1$, which starts with an n-tuple T. Let R be the generating LFSR of **S** with fed-in connections, and let R_i denote the contents of R after i-1 shifts, starting with the initial contents $R_1 = (1000 ... 0)$. Let $\underline{R}_i$ denote the 'reflected' R_i (i.e., writing R_i in reversed order) . The value of the i-th bit of **S** is $T \cdot \underline{R}_i$ (scalar product).

The above property is actually a re-statement of Conclusion 4.3, and an explicit proof will not be given here. We clarify it by an example. The contents of the LFSR of Fig. 4.6a after 4 shifts, starting with the initial contents $R_1 = (1000)$ is $R_5 = (1100)$, and $\underline{R}_5 = (0011)$. Bit #5 of the sequence $S = (00100011110\underline{1}1011)$, which is underlined, is $T \cdot \underline{R}_5 = (1011) \cdot (0011) = 0$.

In order to find bit #6 of the above sequence S, we can either perform the operation $(1011) \cdot \underline{R}_6$ or the operation $(0101) \cdot \underline{R}_5$. (Note that (0101) is the 4-tuple that starts in S at place #2.) This clarifies the following principle: in order to generate the bits of S, starting with bit #5, we generate successive 4-tuples of S, starting with T, and multiply each one by $\underline{R}_5$. Since $\underline{R}_5 = (0011)$, multiplying a 4-tuple X by $\underline{R}_5$ practically means adding the first two bits of X. The circuit depicted in Fig. 4.7 has two outputs. Out 1 is the same sequence S generated by the circuit of Fig. 4.6b. The successive contents of the register are the successive 4-tuples of S. The bits at out 2 are the sums of the first two bits of these successive 4-tuples. Out 2 is therefore the sequence S starting at place #5. This delay between the two outputs is independent of the specific initial state T, with which S starts.

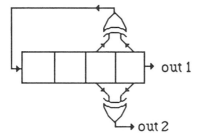

Fig. 4.7 Advancing a maximum-length sequence

The above discussion demonstrated how Property 9 presents a tool for generating advanced versions of maximum-length sequences.

Another way of observing the behavior of the circuit of Fig. 4.7 is the following. Let S_i denote a maximum-length sequence obtained from shifting a maximum-length sequence S, cyclically to the right for i places. If S is the sequence generated at out 1, note that out2 $= S_0 + S_1$. ($S_0 =$ S by definition.) Since it was shown previously that out2 $= S_4$, we have that $S_0 + S_1 = S_4$. This last result shows how Property 9 can be used for generating any desired cyclic shift of a maximum-length sequence S of periodicity $2^n - 1$, by summing some of the shifts $S_0, S_1, \ldots, S_{n-1}$.

Conclusion 4.4 Let S be a maximum-length sequence of periodicity $2^n -$ 1. Let S_i denote the sequence obtained from shifting S cyclically to the right for i places, and let Y denote a matrix whose i-th row, i = 0, 1, 2, ... n $-$ 1, is S_i. Let R be the generating LFSR of S with fed-in connections, and let R_j denote the contents of R after j $-$ 1 shifts, starting with the initial contents $R_1 = (1000 \ldots 0)$. Then $S_{j-1} = R_j \cdot Y$.

CHAPTER 5
SINGLE BURST ERROR CORRECTION

5.1 The Definition of a Burst Error

Until now we have treated the case of a single error occurring in a transmitted code word. In practice, more than one error can occur in a block, in which case we need multiple error correcting codes. The case with which we are concerned in this chapter is a specific occurrence of multiple errors found very frequently in practice.

The causes for error generation in a transmitted signal are usually external interference such as lightning, sparks from ignition systems of motorcars or high tension wires, and fading in the atmosphere. All these kinds of interference have one thing in common — they occur for a short duration, followed by relatively long periods of quiet (as compared with the duration of the interference) only subsequently to occur again. When considering the effect of this phenomenon on the error behavior of transmitted signals, we observe that the errors occur in groups, with a gap between two such consecutive groups. Each group of errors corresponds to the occurrence of a short period of interference of the kind described above, and the period with no errors corresponds to a quiet transmission channel. These groups are called **bursts** of errors. Errors also occur in groups in words that are stored on magnetic media. We will show how to design codes that will enable the correction of a single burst error occurring in a transmitted or stored code word. A class of burst error correcting codes, known as the Reed-Solomon codes, is used, for example in compact disk technology. A separate section in this chapter discusses these codes.

A basic principle in information theory states that the more we know about the behavior of the errors that we have to correct, the simpler are the codes that we have to construct in order to combat these errors. In our case, based on the knowledge that errors come in bursts, the error correcting codes are simpler than general purpose multiple error correcting codes. Our codes should be used, however, only in those cases where we *know* that our channel is bursty (based on intensive measurements), for otherwise our codes are useless.

A basic parameter that we have to consider when designing any burst error correcting code is the length of the burst to be corrected. This length indicates the size (in bits) of the region within which the errors are confined. This is demonstrated by the following example in which b indicates a correct bit and x indicates an erroneous bit:

This example will be modified later. It was given simply in order to have a sample of the problem.

Based on the above example it can already be observed that if we talk about a burst of length t, it does not necessarily mean that *all* the t bits are erroneous. We just mean that all the errors are *confined to t consecutive places* where, for example, only the first and last bits may be erroneous. Here we start to touch on a very delicate point. We have just defined a burst to be of length t if all the errors are confined to t consecutive places. Take now, for example, the block bxbxbbb, where x denotes an erroneous bit. According to what we said, we have here a burst of length 3. However, we also have here a burst of length 4 since the two errors are confined to the first 4 places, out of which only two are in error. (It is not defined that a burst should start or end with an error.) We also have here a burst of length 5, 6, or 7. So the question is: What is the length of this burst? A similar question can be asked when treating the case where only a single bit within a block is erroneous. We can say that we have there a burst of length 1. However, we also have there a burst of length 2, 3, 4, etc. (where only one bit within the burst is erroneous). Also, take again the block bxbxbbb. Is this a single burst? Perhaps there are *two* bursts of length 1, or one burst of length 2 (covering the first two bits of which only one is in error) and another burst of length one, two, three, or four.

The above discussion was not intended to confuse, but rather to sharpen the discussion. We can clear the confusion by stating the following: given a received vector with some errors in it, it is meaningless to ask whether we have here a burst, or what is the length of the burst, or how many bursts we have. The key to designing a single burst error correcting code is *to decide in advance* that we wish to deal with a single burst of length t. This means that we will construct a code such that if the errors in a transmitted code word are all confined to t consecutive places, we will be able to correct them.

5.2   *Single Burst Error Detection*

Let V = (a b c d e f g h i j k m) be a vector whose elements satisfy the following equations:

$$
\begin{aligned}
(1) \quad & a + e + i = 0 \\
(2) \quad & b + f + j = 0 \\
(3) \quad & c + g + k = 0 \\
(4) \quad & d + h + m = 0
\end{aligned}
$$

The above four parity equations, that the elements of V should satisfy, indicate that V can be constructed by attaching four parity bits to an information vector of length 8.

The 3 bits in each of the equations are four places apart in V. In other words, if two bits appear in the same equation, they must be at least five places apart in V. Suppose that we invert some bits of V, where the inverted bits are all confined to four consecutive places. We then have that each inverted bit will affect a different equation, causing its right-hand side to have value 1. Also, since any bit of V appears in some equation (the four equations cover all the 12 bits), it follows that the number of equations whose right-hand side will have a value 1 equals the number of inverted bits. We then have that if a burst error of length four or less is introduced into V, the error is detected. Moreover, the number of 1 elements in the error syndrome equals the number of erroneous bits.

Example Let us invert the values of f, g, and i. Since originally we had that $b + f + j = 0$, $c + g + k = 0$, and $a + b + i = 0$, we now have that $b + f + j = 1$, $c + g + k = 1$, and $a + e + i = 1$. The fourth equation has not changed since the bits d, h, m were not touched.

We now generalize the above idea to the case where we want to detect a burst of a general length t occurring in a transmitted code word in which we have k information bits. The k information bits are encoded into a code word of length k + t by attaching t parity bits. The task of these parity bits is to form a code word having the following property: the sum of all the bits that are t places apart, starting with the first bit, should be 0. The sum of all the bits that are t places apart, starting with the second bit, should be 0, etc; until we sum all the bits that are t places apart, starting with the (t – 1)th bit. (This sum should also be 0.)

For example, take the case where k = 13, t = 5. Here we will convert an information vector of length 13 into a code word of length 18. This code word will have the following properties:

1. The sum of the bits in places #1, 6, 11, 16 equals 0.
2. The sum of the bits in places #2, 7, 12, 17 equals 0.
3. The sum of the bits in places #3, 8, 13, 18 equals 0.
4. The sum of the bits in places #4, 9, 14 equals 0.
5. The sum of the bits in places #5, 10, 15 equals 0.

Our code can be systematic by selecting the parity bits to be bits 14, 15, 16, 17, 18. Each one of them appears in a different sum and can always be selected such that this sum equals 0.

Note that in the above example the length of the code word was not a product of the burst length (which was the case with the first example). However, for convenience as well as for practical purposes, we assume from now onward that *the length of the code word is a product of the burst length.* It is also important to note that the number of parity bits

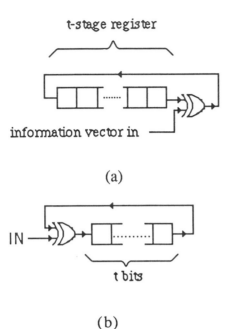

(a)

t bits

(b)

Fig. 5.1 Burst error detection circuitry: a) encoder; b) decoder

that enables the detection of a burst error of length t is t, where *this number is independent of the length of the information vector.*

The preceding descriptions suggest the encoding/decoding circuitry depicted in Fig. 5.1 for detecting burst errors of length t. The parity bits generated by the encoder equal the sum of information bits that appear t places apart in the information vector. The decoder adds those bits in a received message that are t places apart. Its contents form the error syndrome.

5.3 The Connection between the Burst Pattern and Cyclic Shifts of the Error Syndrome

Definition **The pattern of a burst error of length t** is a binary vector of length t whose 1 elements correspond in location to that of the erroneous bits in the burst, where the first erroneous bit indicates location #1 in the pattern.

Example Consider a (12, 8) code, intended for detecting the occurrence of a burst error of length 4 or less. Denote the received message by $M = (m, n, q, r, s, t, u, v, w, x, y, z)$. If m, n, r are erroneous, then the burst pattern is 1101, since the errors are in the first, second and fourth place, starting with m, whose location is #1. If the erroneous bits are r, s, u, the burst pattern is again 1101 since starting with r, the location of the erroneous bits within the burst is again first, second, and fourth. If u and w are erroneous, then the burst pattern is 1010. If a single bit is in error, the burst pattern is 1000, since the first erroneous bit (which is the only erroneous one) indicates the beginning of the burst according to our definition. Note that in a code designed for detecting/correcting a burst of length t *or less*, the burst pattern is always of length t, ending sometimes with 0's.

Consider the case where errors occur at the end of the message and are confined to less than t places. For example y and z in the message M are erroneous. In this case the burst pattern is 1100, meaning that we add artifically extra 0's in order to have a pattern of length t. We always keep the rule that the first erroneous bit in a received message determines the starting point of the burst. This means of course that *the burst pattern always starts with 1.*

Shifting the message M = (m, n, q, r, s, t, u, v, w, x, y, z) into a decoder of the form depicted in Fig. 5.1b, yields the error syndrome S = (s0, s1, s2, s3) where

$$s0 = m + s + w$$
$$s1 = n + t + x$$
$$s2 = q + u + y$$
$$s3 = r + v + z$$

Table 5.1 lists possible erroneous bits in M (falling within a burst of length 4), their corresponding burst pattern, and the effect of the errors on the values of s0, s1, s2, s3. The table exhibits a major issue regarding burst error detection. *The error syndrome is a cyclic shift of the burst pattern.* Further details regarding this phenomenon are treated next.

Erroneous bits in M	Burst pattern	s0	s1	s2	s3
m, n, q, r	(1 1 1 1)	1	1	1	1
q, r, s, t	(1 1 1 1)	1	1	1	1
q, r, t	(1 1 0 1)	0	1	1	1
t, w	(1 0 0 1)	1	1	0	0
u, x	(1 0 0 1)	0	1	1	0
y	(1 0 0 0)	0	0	1	0

Table 5.1   Correspondence among erroneous bits in M, the burst pattern and the generated error syndrome

5.4 The Connection between the Location of a Burst Error and the Amount of Cyclic Shift between the Burst Pattern and the Error Syndrome

Definition **The location of a burst error within a message** is the index of the first erroneous bit.

(The first place in the received message has location index 0.)

Fig. 5.2 depicts a received message M' = (a b c d e f g h i j k m n p q r s t u v w x y z) of length 24. Its transmitted version M was a code word of a (24, 18) code. The six parity bits were attached for the purpose of detecting the occurrence of a burst error of length 6 or less. We consider the cases where M' was obtained from M by introducing into M five possible burst errors, denoted as I, II, III, IV, V. The locations of these bursts are indicated in the figure, as well as their pattern. The pattern

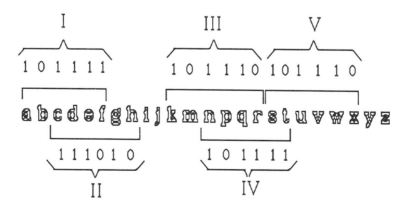

Fig. 5.2   A received message of length 24, with several different error bursts

denoted as I means, for example, that the bits a, c, d, e, f are erroneous. Burst patterns I and IV are the same, as are III and V, but occur in different places.

Only one of these bursts can occur at a particular time. The purpose of drawing the five of them is to analyze the effect of each of them separately.

Table 5.2 lists the relation among the burst patterns, their location within the received message, and the generated syndromes. We observe here again the fact that was already demonstrated by Table 5.1. The syndrome is a cyclic shift of the burst pattern (including the case where the shift is 0, meaning that the syndrome is identical to the burst pattern). For pattern I the shift is 0. For burst II the shift is two places to the left, meaning that the syndrome has to be shifted two places to the left in order to coincide with the burst pattern. For burst III we

Burst #	Pattern	Burst Location	Error Syndrome
I	101111	0	101111
II	111010	2	101110
III	101110	10	111010
IV	101111	12	101111
V	101110	16	111010

Table 5.2 Relation among burst patterns, their location, and the generated error syndrome

have to shift the error syndrome cyclically four places to the left in order to get the burst pattern. For burst IV the shift is zero, and for burst V the shift is four.

We summarize in Table 5.3 the location of each of the five bursts, as well as the amount that the error syndrome should be shifted to the left in order to coincide with the burst pattern.

There is a direct relation between the numbers in the second and third row Table 5.3. The numbers in the third row are obtained by taking the corresponding numbers in the second row, dividing them by 6 and taking the remainder. After this operation a 0 in the second row yields a 0 in the third row, 2 yields 2 (dividing 2 by 6 yields 2 as a remainder), 10 yields 4, 12 yields 0, and 16 yields 4.

Notation The remainder obtained after dividing a number m by the number n is denoted by **m mod n**.

Burst	I	II	III	IV	V
Location	0	2	10	12	16
Amount of shift	0	2	4	0	4

Table 5.3 Summary of the relation between the burst location
and the amount of shift of the error syndrome

Example Dividing 16 by 6 yields 4 as a remainder. Using the above notation we say that 16 mod 6 = 4. More examples:

100 mod 9 = 1,   20 mod 5 = 0,   27 mod 7 = 6,   38 mod 8 = 6.

Conclusion 5.1 Let C be a burst error detection code. Let t denote the length of the burst to be detected and let the length of a code word be divisible by t.   Let x denote the location of a burst error within a transmitted message. If p denotes the burst pattern and s denotes the error syndrome that results from the burst, then p is obtained by shifting s cyclically to the left for x mod t places.

We clarify Conclusion 5.1 once more by considering the case n = 100, t = 10. Let the burst (of length 10) start in a message (of length 100) in location #87. If p is the pattern of this burst and s is the resulting error syndrome (both p and s are 10 bits long), then p is obtained by shifting s cyclically to the left 7 times (87 mod 10 = 7).

5.5 Conditions under Which It Is Possible to Detect the Exact Burst Pattern

Table 5.4 lists all the possible error syndromes corresponding to three specific burst patterns of length 5. These patterns are characterized by the fact that the errors are confined to the first 3 places. The possible error syndromes are all the possible cyclic shifts of the burst pattern.

burst pattern	possible error syndrome
1 0 1 0 0	1 0 1 0 0
	0 1 0 1 0
	0 0 1 0 1
	1 0 0 1 0
	0 1 0 0 1
1 1 0 0 0	1 1 0 0 0
	0 1 1 0 0
	0 0 1 1 0
	0 0 0 1 1
	1 0 0 0 1
1 0 0 0 0	1 0 0 0 0
	0 1 0 0 0
	0 0 1 0 0
	0 0 0 1 0
	0 0 0 0 1

Table 5.4   Some burst patterns of length 5 in which the errors are confined to the first three places, and all the possible corresponding error syndromes

Note now a very important fact that can be shown to be true for all cases: *out of the five cyclic shifts of a pattern, there is only one starting with a single 1 and ending with two 0's. This shift is the 0 shift; that is, it is the pattern itself.*

This means that it is possible to recover the exact form of a burst pattern **p** *of length 3*, by using a code that is intended for detecting bursts *of lengh 5*. This is done by shifting the error sydrome (of length 5) cyclically until it starts with a 1 and ends with two 0's. Such a position is unique and its first three bits equal the burst pattern **p**. If x is the location of the first erroneous bit in a received message, where the length of the message is a multiple of 5, then based on Conclusion 5.1, the process of recovering the burst pattern **p** yields also x mod 5. (Simply count how many times you have to shift to the left the syndrome until you get a 1 at the beginning and two 0's at the end.) This result can be generalized as follows:

Conclusion 5.2 Let C be a burst error detection code. Let u denote the length of the burst to be detected, and let the length of a code word be divisible by u. If the length of the burst that actually occurs in a transmitted message does not exceed [(u+1)/2], then it is possible to detect the exact burst pattern. Also it is possible to calculate x mod u, for x denoting the burst location.

Knowing the burst pattern, the only other thing that we have to know in order to correct the errors is x. The conditions stated in Conclusion 5. 2 already enable us to know x mod u. Next it is shown what else we need in order to recover x completely.

5.6   A Way of Recovering the Location of a Burst Error

5.6.1 The Chinese Remainder Theorem and Its Application to Burst Error Correction

The Chinese Remainder Theorem

Let p and q be two relatively prime numbers. (The largest number by which they are both divisible is 1.) If x is restricted to the range between 0 and pq − 1, then by knowing the values of x mod p and x mod q it is possible to recover x uniquely.

The theorem also states a method for recovering x from x mod p and x mod q, that we shall not give here. (It should also be mentioned that the theorem has a more general form. For simplicity we adopted here a special case.)

Example   3 and 8 are relatively prime. Given that x mod 3 = 2 and x mod 8 = 4, the unique solution for x is x = 20.
Another example x mod 5 = 1, x mod 3 = 0. The solution is x = 6.

Conclusion 5.2 showed us how can we get x mod u, where x is the location within the received message of a burst of length t, for u = 2t − 1. In view of the Chinese Remainder Theorem, the complete recovery of x is possible if another value of the form x mod v is known. If u and v are relatively prime, then we can solve x uniquely as long as the length of the message does not exceed u·v. (Since the index of the first location in the message is 0, the length u·v ensures that no location index exceeds u·v − 1, thus ensuring that x has a unique solution.)

In order to have another value of the form x mod v, we generate the code word that will satisfy a further set of parity equations. (Being able to detect burst error of length u already means that the sum of all the bits in a code word that are u places apart, starting with bits #0, 1, ..., u − 1, should be 0.) This further set indicates that *the sum of all the bits that are v places apart, starting with bits #0, 1, ..., v − 1, should also be 0.*

In practice the value of v is selected to be t itself (where u = 2t − 1).

Example For u = 5 and v = 3 we require that the bits of the code word (abcdefghijkmnpq) satisfy the following equations:

$$a+f+k \ = \ 0$$
$$b+g+m = \ 0$$
$$c+h+n \ = \ 0$$
$$d+i+p \ = \ 0$$
$$e+j+q \ = \ 0$$

The code word should also satisfy the equations:
$$a+d+g+j+n \ \ = \ 0$$
$$b+e+h+k+p \ \ = \ 0$$
$$c+f+i+m+q \ \ = \ 0$$

5.6.2 A Complete Error Correction Procedure

We now show a complete error correction procedure. For ease of explanation we will base the following discussion on the specific case where u = 5 and t = 3. Let M' = (101101000100010) be a received message. Its transmitted version M satisfied the eight equations listed above. A burst error of a length not exceeding 3 was then introduced into M, forming M'.

Let x denote the location of the burst error in M'. Based on Conclusion 5.2, we can recover from the error syndrome the pattern of the burst as well as x mod 5. The receiver starts the decoding process by calculating the syndrome S = (s0, s1, s2, s3, s4). The bits of the syndrome are obtained by summing those bits of M' that are 5 places apart:

$$s0 = 1 + 1 + 0 = 0$$
$$s1 = 0 + 0 + 0 = 0$$
$$s2 = 1 + 0 + 0 = 1$$
$$s3 = 1 + 0 + 1 = 0$$
$$s4 = 0 + 1 + 0 = 1$$

The receiver must now take the error syndrome (00101) and shift it cyclically to the left until it starts with a 1 and end with two 0's. This is obtained by shifting the syndrome cyclically two places to the left, resulting the pattern (10100). The burst pattern is 101 and x mod 5 = 2.

We now calculate the syndrome $Z = (z0, z1, z2)$. The bits of this syndrome are obtained by summing those bits of M' that are 3 places apart:

$$z0 = 1 + 1 + 0 + 1 + 0 = 1$$
$$z1 = 0 + 0 + 0 + 0 + 1 = 1$$
$$z2 = 1 + 1 + 0 + 0 + 0 = 0$$

It is already known that the burst pattern is 101, from the above result. Let us now apply Conclusion 5.1. According to that conclusion, the amount by which we must shift the syndrome (110) to the left in order to get the pattern (101) equals x mod 3. Shifting (110) cyclically once to the left yields (101), meaning that x mod 3 = 1. The two error syndromes have now given the equations: x mod 5 = 2; x mod 3 = 1. The unique solution to x is x = 7. We have therefore recovered x from the two error syndromes, where the burst pattern was already recovered from the first error syndrome. Knowing the location x and the pattern, we can now correct the errors. They are in places 7 and 9 in M' (where the counting starts from the left and the first bit is #0).

The technique demonstrated above for correcting a burst of length 3 can be stated generally as follows: A burst of length t can be corrected within a code word of length u·t where u = 2t – 1. This is possible if the code word has a structure that enables the independent detection of bursts of length u and t. Detection of a burst of length u (in which the errors are confined to t places) will enable the recovery of the burst pattern and x mod u, where x is the burst location. This is done by means of Conclusion 5.2. We also apply the independent scheme intended for detecting a burst of length t. Since we already know the burst pattern, we apply Conclusion 5.1 and recover x mod t. From x mod u and x mod t, we recover x. Since we already know the burst pattern, recovering its location permits a complete correction.

5.6.3 Hardware Techniques for Recovering the Burst Pattern and Its Location Out of the Error Syndromes

Next we show a simple hardware technique for recovering the burst pattern and its location x. The principles applied here will be based on the preceding discussion. Let S and Z denote respectively the error syndromes of length u and t, generated from the received message. We know that the number of places that these syndromes have to be shifted cyclically to the left in order to yield the burst pattern is x mod u and x mod t. Based on the definition of modular arithmetic it follows that if we shift each one of them cyclically to the left *for x places*, the shifted Z will equal the burst pattern and the shifted S will have the burst pattern on its left t places.

Based on this principle we can formulate a simple way of recovering the burst pattern and its location out of the two syndromes. We simply shift them cyclically to the left until the left t bits of the shifted S equal the shifted Z, where they both start with a 1. The burst pattern is then the shifted Z and the number of shifts that yielded this situation is the burst location x.

As an example take the case where u = 5 and t = 3. Suppose that S = (00101) and Z = (110). Listed below are the forms of successive cyclic shifts to the left of S and Z.

Shift	S	Z
0	00101	110
1	01010	101
2	10100	011
3	01001	110
4	10010	101
5	00101	011
6	01010	110
7	10100	101

After 7 shifts we have arrived at the described situation. The burst pattern for this case is then (101) and its location within the received message is 7.

5.6.4 Clarifying Remarks

We conclude this section by stating two important remarks:

1. It was stated that the code word should independently satisfy the conditions that enable the detection of bursts of length u and t, where u = 2t − 1. The value 2t − 1 is the *minimum* value that u should have. Any value higher than this will also enable the correction of a burst of length t, provided that the length of a code word does not exceed ut. (u and t should also keep their relative primality.) Because of efficiency considerations, we assume here, and also later, the case where u equals its lower bound.

2. The burst correction scheme treated above is valid only in cases where the burst pattern, of length t, is not periodic (i.e., it does not consist of a section that repeats itself). If the pattern is periodic, then there are several cyclic shifts that yield the same pattern. (Take, for example, the case where the pattern is all 1. It equals itself under any cyclic shift.) We thus have a case where the described technique for recovering x mod t will not yield a unique result since the same pattern is obtained after various shifts. In order to overcome this difficulty, we restrict here the value of t to being a prime number. This will ensure that the pattern will not be periodic unless it is all 1, in which case we really cannot correct it. Bear in mind, however, that the treatment of burst error correction codes given here is intended purely for introducing the basic principles. There is no practical code that is based entirely on the described technique. In more sophisticated schemes difficulties like the above are, of course, overcome.

5.7 Burst Error Correction Circuitry – The Decoder

The decoder described next enables an automatic correction of a burst
error of length t, based on the principles of the Chinese remainder
theorem. This includes the recovery of the burst pattern and its position
inside a received message. Figure 5.3 depicts such a decoder for the
case u = 5, t = 3. It consists of three independent registers: R1, R2, and
R3. The received signal of length 3·5 = 15, is shifted simultaneously into
these registers, where R1 stores the message. R2 and R3 are our
standard syndrome generators of length 5 and 3.

For clarification, take the message   M' = (101101000100010)
discussed before, and shift it into the circuit. (The bit shifted in first is
the bit on the left of M'.) The final contents of R2 and R3 are (110)
and (00101) respectively. In order to correct M' we have to recover the

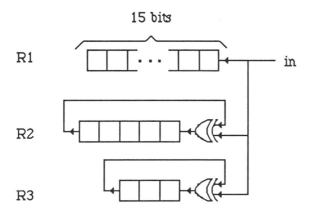

Fig. 5.3 Correcting a single burst error of length t = 3 in a block of
length $2t^2 - t = 15$: the decoder

burst pattern and its location x. We now apply the technique described in section 5.6.3. We shift R2 and R3 until the contents of the left three stages of R2 equals that of R3, where the left bit is 1. (Additional circuitry should be added here for detecting this situation.) The contents of R2 is then the burst error and the number of shifts is the location of the first erroneous bit in M'. Note that when drawing Fig. 5.3 we did not use the convention of right-shift LFSRs, and the input is on the right. This was made in order that the circuit will correspond to the preceding explanations. It will later be "reflected" back to the normal conventions.

The errors in M' can be automatically corrected if M' is shifted out, bit by bit, from register R1 together with the cyclic shift of the other two registers. The number of shifts when we arrive at the described situation (in which the contents of the left three stages of R2 equals that of R3, and the left bit is 1), equals the location x of the first erroneous bit in M'. Note that if the bits of M' are shifted out at the same rate as R2 and R3 shift, then *the x-th bit of M' is exactly the one shifted out when the described situation is detected.* Since R2 contains at that time the burst pattern, a complete error correction is performed by adding the contents of R2, bit by bit, to the three bits shifted out of R1.

5.8 Burst Error Correction Circuitry – The Encoder

Consider now an encoding circuit corresponding to the decoder of Fig. 5.3. The syndrome generator consists of the two registers connected in parallel, and ways of constructing the encoding LFSR were given in detail in section 4.4. The feedback connections of our encoding LFSR can then be determined by the operation:

$$(1001) \cdot \begin{matrix} 100001000 \\ 010000100 \\ 001000010 \\ 000100001 \end{matrix} = (100101001)$$

The left eight bits of the resultant vector (100101001) indicate the feedback connections of an encoding LFSR. This encoder is depicted in Fig. 5.4.

Note that when describing the above process we were very cautious. We said that the obtained encoder is *an* encoder corresponding to the decoder of Fig. 5.3. We did not say that it is *the* encoder. By this we mean that there is another LFSR, shorter than the one above, that is an encoder of our code. In order to understand why, let us go back to the vectors **v1**, **v2**, and **v3** of section 4.4. The only requirement was that **v3** will consist of linear shifts of both **v1** and **v2**. One way of obtaining such a **v3** was to perform the vector-matrix multiplication described. However, this is not the only way of obtaining a vector consisting of linear shifts of both **v1** and **v2**. In the specific case treated here we have **v1** = (100100000) and **v2** = (100001000). It can be verified by inspection that the vector **v3** = (111001110) also consists of the sum of linear shifts of both **v1** and **v2**.

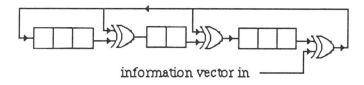

information vector in

Fig. 5.4 An encoder corresponding to the decoder of Fig. 5.3

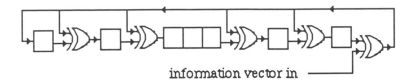

Fig. 5.5   Another possible encoder

The   feedback connections of the LFSR corresponding to **v3** are indicated by its leftmost seven bits. This LFSR is depicted in Fig. 5.5.

The burst error correction code whose decoder is depicted in Fig. 5.3 has code words of length 15. The Chinese Remainder Theorem tells us that a burst error cannot be corrected if the code word is longer than 15. On the other hand, the two encoders of Fig. 5.4 and 5.5, that are both suitable for our code, have different lengths. Since the length of the encoding register determines the number of parity bits, it follows that the code generated by the encoder of Fig. 5.4 is of dimensions (15, 7), and that generated by the other register is of dimensions (15, 8). The second code is more efficient: it encodes an extra information bit, offering the same error correction capability. Also the value of Pu - defined as the periodicity of an LFSR related to the state (1000...0) - is 27 for the first encoder and 15 for the second. Based on Proposition 4.3, the second code is cyclic. The first one is not cyclic, as can be demonstrated by taking, for example, the code word (000000100101001). Shifting this code word one place cyclically to the right yields a vector that is not a code word.

5.9 Using a Cyclic Hamming Code for Detecting Burst Errors

Fig. 5.6 depicts a communication scenario where M = (a b c d e f g) is a received message whose transmitted version was a code word C = (a x y z e f g). The message M contains a burst error of length 3, confined to places 2, 3, and 4 (counting from the left). M consists then of the sum of C and the error vector E, where E contains the burst pattern (i j k) in places 2, 3, and 4, and the rest of its elements are 0.

We take now the case where C is a code word of the code whose parity matrix is H' (of chapter 3). The syndrome generator of this code is depicted in Fig. 5.7 which is a redrawn version of Fig. 3.2.

Because M – C + E and because of the linearity of R1, it follows that the contents of R1, after shifting the message M into it, equals the contents obtained by shifting only E into it (since the addend C is a code word yielding an "all 0" contents).

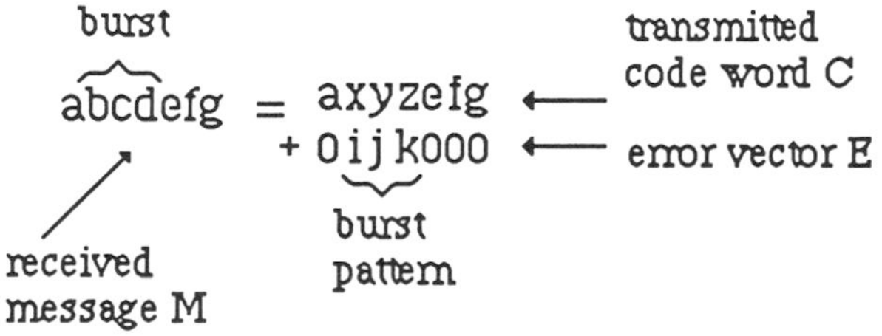

Fig. 5.6 A basic communication scenario involving a burst error

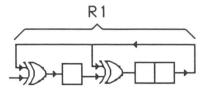

Fig. 5.7   Fig. 3.2 redrawn

Consider now the effect of shifting the error vector E into R1. (We are
entitled to consider only the shifting of E, provided that our final analysis
will be based on at least seven shifts, since we actually shift M into R1,
and the effect of C is filtered out only after seven shifts.) After 6 shifts the
contents of R1 is the burst pattern (i j k). After the seventh shift, when E
is shifted completely into R1, the contents changes and is not the burst
pattern any more. This contents is the error syndrome.   Due to the
linearity of the register, once its contents is nonzero, it can never get to an
"all 0" contents, no matter how many times we shift it. The final contents
of the LFSR, after E is completely shifted, is therefore nonzero since it
was nonzero after the sixth shift.. In other words, the existence of a burst
error of length 3 or less will always generate a nonzero syndrome,
enabling error detection. This consideration is independent of the fact that
our specific LFSR happens to have maximum periodicity, leading us to
the following general conclusion.

Conclusion 5.3   Any code generated by an LFSR of length n can be used
for detecting the occurrence of a burst error of length n or less in a
transmitted code word.

The issue considered next is the possibility of devising LFSR's
intended for burst error detection, having also the property that the code

words generated by them have an even Hamming weight. This will enable the detection of an odd number of errors (as was trivially shown in the first chapter), beside burst error detection. Since such LFSR's were adopted as international standards, as will be shown later, it was decided to treat them here specifically.

We showed in chapter 4 that if a code is generated by an LFSR of length n, then the first n bits of the first row of the generating matrix G of the code correspond to the feedback connections of the generating LFSR. These n bits are followed by a 1, and the rest of the bits in the row are 0. It then follows that if the number of stages in the generating LFSR, into which the feedback line is fed, is odd, then the first row of G has an even number of 1's.

Turn now to Proposition 4.1. It states that all the code words of a code consist of the sum of linear shifts of the first row of the generating matrix G of the code. All these shifts have the same Hamming weight as the first row, and all have therefore the same parity. If they all have parity 0, like in our case, then any sum of them (i.e., any code word) also has parity 0. It follows that if C is a code generated by an LFSR having the property that the number of stages into which the feedback line is fed, is odd, then all the code words of C have parity 0.

Conclusion 5.4   It is always possible to detect the existence of an odd number of errors occurring in a code word of a code C whose generating LFSR has the property that the number of stages into which the feedback line is fed, is odd.

Some specific LFSR's used for generating burst error detection codes were accepted as international standards. The three LFSR's depicted in Fig. 5.8 all have an odd number of stages connected to the feedback line. Their error detection capability may be determined from Conclusions 5.3 and 5.4.

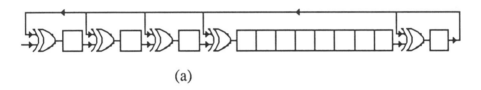

(a)

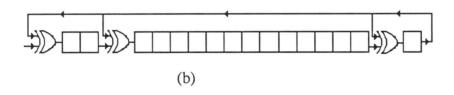

(b)

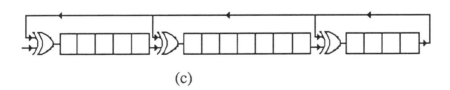

(c)

Fig. 5.8 Three LFSR's accepted as international standards:
(a) CRC-12; (b) CRC-16; (c) CRC-CCITT

5.10 Using a Cyclic Hamming Code for Correcting Burst Errors Based on Knowing the Burst Pattern

We turn back to Fig. 5.6 and the discussion following it. It was argued that shifting M into R1 is equivalent to shifting only E into R1. Whereas in the preceding section we did not make a use of the fact that R1 has maximum periodicity (this property is irrelevant for burst error *detection* analysis), we shall use this property here, when analyzing the burst error *correction* capability of the code generated by R1.

When shifting E into R1, the contents of R1 after 6 shifts was shown to be the burst pattern (i j k). Due to the periodicity of R1, *if we keep on shifting it seven more times, we get the burst pattern back.* (We will not get this pattern before these additional 7 shifts are over since this LFSR has diferent contents during seven sucessive shifts, if the initial contents is not "all 0.")

Generally, if we somehow know the burst pattern but do not know its location within M (whose transmitted version was a code word of our code), the following procedure applies. After loading M into R1 (7 shifts), continue shifting until R1 contains the burst pattern. If the additional number of shifts is k, then the burst starts at place $7 - k$, counting from the left. (If the burst is confined to places 0, 1, 2, the scheme is still valid. Explain why.)

The process stated above is actually a generalization of the single error correction process of a cyclic Hamming code, treated already in chapter 3. In that case we know that the "burst pattern" is (100). Here we argue that the knowledge of *any* burst pattern (of a proper length) enables the correction of the errors.

Consider now the case of a message P of length 7k, for some integer k, having the property that after being shifted into register R1 of Fig. 5.7 the final contents is all 0. Let Q be obtained by introducing a burst error of length 3 or less into P, where the burst starts at place i. Again assume that we know the burst pattern. Based on the periodicity of R1 and on the preceding discussion (concerning the message M of length 7) we can conclude the following: if Q is shifted into R1, and R1 is shifted further for j places until it contains the burst pattern, then i mod 7 = 7 − j. This observation forms the basis of the code introduced in the next section.

For tutorial purposes we now repeat the same considerations given above, where instead of considering LFSR manipulations, we treat the parity matrix of the code. The following can be skipped, however (until the beginning of section 5.11), without loss of continuity.

The parity matrix of our specific code is H'. Let H_j' be the matrix obtained by shifting the rows of H' cyclically upward j places. As our code is cyclic (i.e., the cyclic shift of a code word is also a code word), we have that $C \cdot H_j' = 0$. It then follows that $M \cdot H_j'$ yields the sum of those rows of H_j' whose location is that of the errors in M. Note that although we shifted the rows of H' and not the code word C, the product $C \cdot H_j'$ yields the same result that would have been obtained from multiplying a cyclic shift of C by H'.

Let the burst error be confined to places #i, i + 1, i + 2 in M, where the bits are counted starting from the left. (The first bit is #0). Then M · $H'_{(7-i)}$ yields the burst pattern. This follows from the fact that H' starts with a unit matrix of dimension 3 x 3. $H'_{(7-i)}$ then has this unit matrix in places #i, i + 1, i + 2, and $M \cdot H'_{(7-i)}$ actually yields as a result the burst pattern multiplied by the unit matrix. That is, the result is the pattern. (Note that if i=0, i.e., the errors are confined to the first 3 places in M, then $H'_{(7-i)} = H_7' = H'$, and our argument is also valid here.)

Our error correction scheme is now clear. If we know the burst pattern, then we multiply M by cyclic shifts of H' until we get the burst pattern. The error location can then be recovered from the number of the shifts.

5.11 The Fire Code

We treat the decoder depicted in Fig. 5.9. Let us take the (35, 27) code whose code words have the property that after being fed to this decoder, both R2 and R3 contain only 0's.

Note that R3 is the syndrome generator of the Hamming code shown in Fig. 5.7. Each code word of our code satisfies the following condition: the sum of all the bits that are 5 places apart, starting with place #0, #1, #2, #3, #4, yield 0. Because of this general property R2 contains 0's when the code word is loaded into the system. The fact that R3 also contains 0's when the shift is completed, means the following: construct a matrix M by repeating the matrix H' of section 3.1 five times

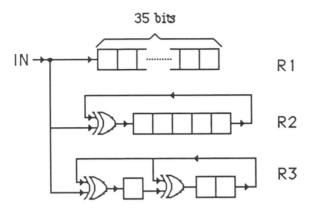

Fig. 5.9   A proposed decoder

one below the other. (M then has three columns and thirty-five rows.) Any code word C of our code then has the property C·M = 0.

Each code word of our new code satisfies eight independent parity checks. This was enabled at the transmitting side by attaching eight parity bits to a given information vector.

Our code enables the correction of a single burst error of length 3 in a block of length 35. To understand why this is so, observe first that with such a burst error, the final contents of R2 enables us to recover the burst pattern as well as x mod 5, where x is the burst location. The justification for this argument is identical to our explanation of the circuit in Fig. 5.3.

After deriving the burst pattern, we apply the technique presented in section 5.10. We continue shifting R3 until we arrive at our known burst

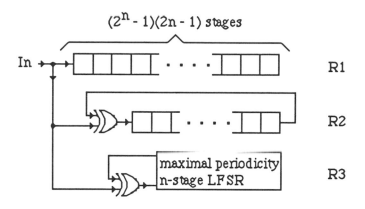

Fig. 5.10 A general Fire code decoder

pattern. This will yield x mod 7. The Chinese Remainder Theorem then guarantees that we can recover x.

The decoder of a general Fire code for $2^n - 1$ and $2n - 1$ relatively prime is depicted in Fig. 5.10. It is a generalization of that depicted in Fig. 5.9, and its validity is based on the same consideration.

The design of the encoding circuits corresponding to our decoders is based again on the details given in section 4.4. We will now treat specifically the encoder of the Fire code whose decoder is depicted in Fig. 5.9. The syndrome generator there consists of the two registers R2 and R3, of length 5 and 3, connected in parallel. The feedback connections of the encoding LFSR corresponding to our decoder can be determined by the operation:

$$
(100001) \cdot
\begin{array}{l}
110100000 \\
011010000 \\
001101000 \\
000110100 \\
000011010 \\
000001101
\end{array}
= (110101101)
$$

The leftmost eight bits of the resultant vector (110101101) indicate the feedback connections of the encoding LFSR. This encoder is depicted in Fig. 5.11.

The two sets of parity equations dictated by the syndrome generators R2 and R3 of Fig. 5.9 are totally independent, unlike the case with the sets of equations dictated by R2 and R3 of Fig. 5.3. This means that the encoder of our Fire code cannot be implemented by an LFSR shorter than the one depicted in Fig. 5.11.

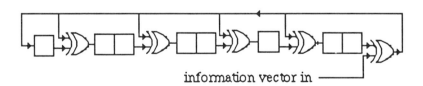

information vector in

Fig. 5.11   The encoder corresponding to the decoder of Fig. 5.9

5.12   Single Character Error Correction   (the RS Code)

5.12.1   Character Error Detection

Sometimes messages are transmitted or stored as blocks of characters. The message M = (100, 001, 011, 101, 110, 111, 010), that will be used in later examples, consists of a block of seven characters, each one of length 3. Some codes were especially designed for correcting errors occurring in received characters. These codes have recently become popular, because of their application in compact disk technology. Here the information is stored in the form of blocks of bytes that are very sensitive to errors.

The specific code selected for use in compact disk technology is the RS (Reed-Solomon) code. The case treated in this text is the one where we assume that only one character can be erroneous within a block.

The RS code is actually a burst error correction code, since we correct multiple bit errors falling within the specified frame of a character. The length of the character is then the length of the burst that should be corrected.

Definition   Let C be a transmitted character, and let C' be its received version. The pattern E = C + C' is called **the character error pattern**.

Although the errors introduced into C are some form of a burst, we had to introduce the above definition in order to distinguish between a character error pattern and burst error pattern. Whereas the second must start by definition with a 1, this is not necessarily the case with the first.

For instance, if C = (110) and C' = (111), then the character error pattern
is (001).

Examine the message M given before, that consists of 21 bits.
Applying burst error correction techniques for correcting character errors
here is much easier than applying such techniques for correcting any burst
of length 3, since we know that the character error pattern starts with bit
#3p and ends with bit #3p + 2, for some integer p.

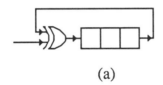

(a)

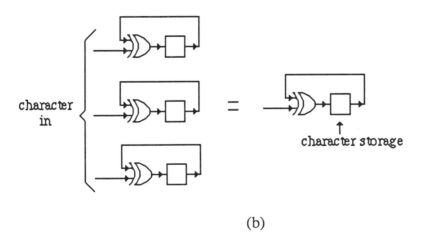

(b)

Fig. 5.12 (a) Burst error detection; (b) character error detection

Fig. 5.12a depicts a burst error detection circuit (for bursts of length 3). Fig. 5.12b depicts a character error detection circuit. A full character of length 3 is fed into this circuit during each shift, where the XOR operation is done between the stored character and the character fed in. The circuit on the right-hand side describes the same behavior and represents the convention to be used in this text.

It can be easily checked that after shifting the message M, listed above, into the circuit of Fig. 5.12b, the contents of the register will be 'all 0'. Let M' be the received version of M. From the material presented earlier in this chapter it follows that if a character is erroneous (i.e., we have an error pattern confined to three successive places, starting with place #3p), then *this contents is the character error pattern.*

Example M' = (100, 001, 011, 101, 111, 111, 010).

M' was obtained by introducing the character error pattern (001) into the fifth character (counting from the left). After shifting M' into either of the circuits depicted in Fig. 5.12, the final contents will be (001).

Detecting burst errors of length t in a received message is enabled by introducing t parity bits into the transmitted message. It follows that *introducing a parity character into a transmitted block of characters enables the recovery of the character error pattern* (in the case of a single erroneous character).

5.12.2 Character Error Correction
The code word in an RS code is a block consisting of $2^n - 1$ characters of

length n. There are two parity characters and $2^n - 3$ information
characters in a code word of a single error correction RS code (that
enables the correction of one erroneous character).   The code is
systematic. For brevity, whenever we mention the RS code from now
on, we mean specifically the single error correction code.

The decoder of our RS code is based on the syndrome generators of
Fig. 5.13. The cells depicted in the figure store entire characters. The
transmitted block of characters has the property that when it is shifted into
the two syndrome generators, both will have a final "all 0" contents.

The functioning of register #1 is explained as follows. There is a
maximum periodicity LFSR of length n associated with an RS code. (A
reminder: n is also the length of the characters, where the transmitted
block consists of $2^n - 1$ characters.) We denote this register by R, where
R_i denotes its contents after i shifts, starting with the initial contents $R_0 =$
(1000 ... 0). There is a matrix Q associated with R. This matrix is the
one described in section 4.1 (Property **c**). It consists of n rows that are

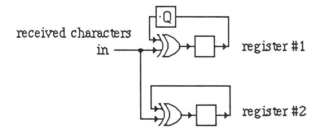

Fig.5.13   The syndrome generators of a single error correction RS code

the sucessivc contents of R, starting with R_1 and ending with R_n. It was

shown that $R_i \cdot Q = R_{i+1}$, for any $0 \le i \le 2^n - 2$.

Referring now to register #1, we observe that its contents is multiplied by Q before it is XORed with the incoming character. That is, (new contents) = (old contents)$\cdot$Q + (incoming character). Since any contents of the register is either 'all 0' or equals some R_i, we find that multiplication by Q yields 0 in the first case and R_{i+1} in the second. For clarification purposes, Table 5.5 lists the successive contents of register #1 for the cases where the messages M and M', given in the preceding examples, are shifted into it. Here n = 3, and the register R is the one depicted in Fig. 3.1. The matrix Q associated with it is:

$$Q = \begin{matrix} 010 \\ 001 \\ 110 \end{matrix}$$

input block M	input block M'
010	010
110	110
101	100
001	111
101	110
101	010
000	101

Table 5.5 Successive contents of register #1 of Fig. 5.13

When considering register #2 of Fig. 5.13, it is recognized as that of Fig. 5.12. It sums the received characters. From the preceding discussions we know that if the sum of the characters of a transmitted block is the character "all 0", and a single-character error occurred during the transmission, then the sum of the received characters yields the character error pattern. For the specific case of the transmitted message M and the received message M' treated above, the sum of the characters is (000) and (001), respectively.

We now explain the error correction procedure of our RS code. A transmitted message M and its received version M' have $2^n - 2$ characters in common, and may differ in one character. Let $E = M + M'$. The error block E consists of 2^n-2 characters that are "all 0" and one character that equals the error pattern. As our code is linear and M is a code word, the contents of the syndrome generators of Fig.5.13 after shifting M' into them is the same as that obtained by shifting only E.

Let the characters of M, M', and E be indexed, where the leftmost character is #0. Let the erroneous character be #i. The error pattern character equals some R_j, where R is the maximum periodicity LFSR associated with our code (based upon which the matrix Q was formed). We now analyze the effect of shifting E into register #1 of Fig. 5.13. We start by shifting in the rightmost character. The contents of the register is 0 until the error pattern is shifted in. At this time the contents of the register is R_j. The register is now shifted a further i times, until the leftmost character is shifted in. The input characters during these i shifts are always 0, and *the circuit generates successive contents of R* (that is the effect of successive multiplications by Q). The final contents of the register is therefore R_{j+i}. At this time the contents of register #2 is the character error pattern R_j. (This effect has already been explained.) To summarize *one register yields R_{j+i}, and the other yields R_j= error pattern.*

A complete correction process of a single erroneous character means recovering both the error pattern and the location of the erroneous character. The process described above directly yields the error pattern. Recovering the error location means the recovery of the index i. Since we know R_j (that is the error pattern) and we know R_{j+i}, a possible way of recovering i is to feed R_j into the register R and to shift it until we get the pattern known to us as R_{j+i}. By counting the number of shifts we get i.

Another way of recovering i is by shifting the register R, starting with the contents R_{j+i}, until we get the contents R_j. The number of shifts in this case is $2^n - i$. This is based on the observation that $(j + i) + (2^n -1 - i) = j + 2^n - 1$. However, due to the periodicity of R, its contents after $j + 2^n-1$ shifts is R_j. Note now that $2^n - 2 - i$ is the location of the erroneous character in E, *counting from the right.* (This is clarified by observing that the rightmost bit is bit #$2^n - 2$ counting from the left, and is bit #0 counting from the right.) We are now ready to explain the error correction circuitry depicted in Fig. 5.14.

The received block that consists of $2^n - 1$ characters is shifted into the three registers. The block is stored in register #3, while the two at the bottom ar e the syndrome generators of Fig. 5.13. During this shift the

received characters in

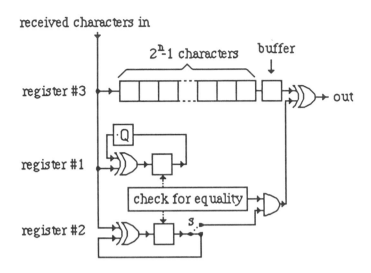

Fig. 5.14 A complete single character correction RS decoder

switch S closes the feedback line of register #2. After the received block
is completely shifted in, switch S connects the contents of register #2 to
the input of an AND gate. This contents is 'all 0' in the case where there
is no error, and the character error pattern in the case where there is an
error. (Note that a complete character enters the AND gate: i.e., this gate
has n+1 single-bit inputs, n of which are the character from the register
and an additional single bit from the circuit "check for equality".) Now
we continue to shift both registers #3 and #1. While characters exit the
circuit, register #1 acts as the register R, generating successive contents
of R starting with R_{j+i}. After 2^n-1-i shifts, the contents of register #1
is R_j. Registers #2 and #1 then have the same contents and the output
from the circuit "check for equality" is 1. The contents of register #2 that
is the error pattern is shifted into the XOR gate and is XORed with the

character now stored in the buffer. Following the counting clarifies that *this character is the erroneous one* and the XOR operation corrects it. In the case where there is no error, the output from the AND gate is always 0, and the received message is shifted unaltered out of register #3.

Example Take the case of the messages M and M' treated before. After M' is shifted into the circuit of Fig. 5.14, the contents of registers #1 and #2 are (101) and (001), respectively. (See Table 5.5 and an example preceding it.) Shifting on register #1, its successive contents are (100), (010), (001). After three shifts we obtain an equality between the contents of the two registers. At this time the erroneous character is shifted into the buffer. (When introducing M', we noted that the erroneous character is located 3 places from the right.) We now XOR it with the error pattern and correct it.

Note that the number of parity characters in M, needed for performing a single-character error correction, is the sum of the lengths of the syndrome generators. This sum is two. That is, out of the $2^n - 1$ characters in m, $2^n - 3$ are information characters and two are parity characters.

We conclude this section by introducing the encoding circuitry of our RS code. Here we have to construct a circuit that satisfies simultaneously the two independent parity constraints imposed by the two syndrome generators of Fig. 5.13. This problem has already been dealt with in section 4.4. We repeat the result stated there: the feedback connections of a LFSR corresponding to two LFSR's connected in parallel are found by the operation $\mathbf{v} \cdot \mathbf{M}$, where $\mathbf{v}$ represents the feedback connections of one

LFSR and the rows of **M** consist of linear shifts of the vector corresponding to the feedback connection of the other LFSR. In the case of the RS code, the LFSR's handle entire characters, and *the feedback connections are not denoted by 0 and 1 but rather by matrices*. For example, the feedback connections of register #2, that appear to be (11), are actually (II), where I is a unit matrix of dimension n x n. By the same token, the feedback connections of register #1 are (QI). In order to find the single LFSR corresponding to the parallel operation of these two registers, we then perform the operation:

$$(I\ I) \cdot \begin{matrix} Q\ I\ 0 \\ 0\ Q\ I \end{matrix} = (Q\ P\ I) \quad \text{where P denotes the matrix I+Q.}$$

The encoder whose feedback connections correspond to (QPI) is depicted in Fig. 5.15. As was indicated above, the number of information characters entering the encoder is $2^n - 3$. The final contents of the following LFSR will form the parity characters attached to the information characters, forming the transmitted codeblock.

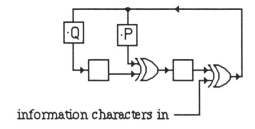

Fig. 5.15 A complete single character correction RS encoder

CHAPTER 6
CONVOLUTIONAL CODES

6.1 Basic Concepts

Until now we were concerned only with block codes, in which the transmitted information always consisted of code words of a prespecified length. Convolutional codes are used in cases where the transmitted information is a contiguous string of bits of undefined length. In order to deal here with the effect of errors, the bit stream is broken in predefined spots where parity bits are inserted, as depicted in Fig. 6.1.

The parity bits are not necessarily equidistant, as shown in the figure. Each equals the sum of a combination of several preceding bits. Throughout the entire encoding process the parity bits are constructed in a fixed prescribed manner. For example P_0 can equal the sum of its three preceding bits. P_1 can equal the sum of the two bits transmitted 2 and 3 clock periods before. P_2 can equal again the sum of its three preceding bits, etc.

Information: ...a b c d e f g h i j k...
Received signal: ...a b c P_0 d e f g P_1 h i j P_3 k...

Fig. 6.1 Inserting parity bits into the transmitted information

There are numerous convolutional codes, intended for dealing with randomly distributed errors, burst errors, or both. (When we say "both" we mean the case where errors appear in bursts, and we also allow a limited number of single errors to occur between bursts.) Because this is an introductory level text, we have chosen a burst error correcting convolutional code known as the "diffuse threshold decoding" code. (We are not going to explain here the meaning of these words.) As far as tutorial purposes are concerned, this code has the following attractive properties:

1. It is one of the most popular codes used presently in commercial equipment.

2. The principles upon which it operates are common to some other codes. Understanding these principles will then provide the reader with a solid background.

3. It is elegant and easy to explain.

When dealing with single burst error-correcting block codes, the relevant parameters are the burst length t and the block length n. We can correct up to t errors occurring in a block of length n, using the restriction that the errors are confined to not more than t consecutive places within the block. When dealing with convolutional codes, the concept "block" does not exist. The burst error correction block codes with which we were dealing had the restriction that only a *single* burst error is allowed in each block. When considering our convolutional code, we have an equivalent restriction indicated by the demand that there must be an error-free region between two successive bursts. This error free region is called a **recovery region**, since the system must recover from the effect of a burst error before being able to treat the next burst. The minimal size of the recovery region depends on the size of the burst to be corrected. In the case of diffuse threshold decoding codes, the minimal size of the recovery region is 3t + 2, where t indicates the maximal length of the burst error that can be corrected.

6.2 Diffuse Threshold Decoding Codes: Encoding Process

The encoder of the diffuse threshold decoding code is depicted in Fig. 6.2. It consists of a shift register, split into three sections. The first two sections are of length t/2, and the third is of length t/2 + 1, for t denoting the length of the burst to be corrected. Note that t should be an even magnitude (for t/2 to be an integer). There is an XOR gate whose four inputs are indicated clearly in the figure. The consecutive outputs of the XOR gate are the parity bits. The inputs to the encoder are the information bits ... I_3 I_2 I_1 fed in sequentially starting with I_1. (Note

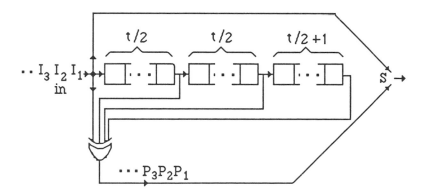

Fig. 6.2   The encoder of the diffuse threshold decoding convolutional codes

that we count from the right since I_1 is the first bit fed into the circuit, then I_2 etc.) The information bits diverge in three directions. They are fed into the shift register, into the XOR gate, and directly to the output.

We explain now the functioning of the switch S and the form of the output. Alternately the switch S connects between the top and bottom channels. By "alternately" we mean that the switch is toggled at double the clock rate at which the information bits are fed in. Therefore, for each information bit fed in, there are *two* bits fed out by the switch and transmitted. This means that the transmission rate is twice the rate of the input. These two bits are the information bit, fed via the top channel, and the parity bit which is the present output of the XOR gate, fed via the bottom channel. For ... $I_3 \ I_2 \ I_1$, being the successive values of the input bits and ... $P_3 \ P_2 \ P_1$, being the successive parity bits generated by the XOR gate, the transmitted output is ... $P_3 \ I_3 \ P_2 \ I_2 \ P_1 \ I_1$.

6.3 Diffuse Threshold Decoding Codes: Decoding Process

Fig. 6.3 depicts a circuit which is the "inverse" of the encoder of

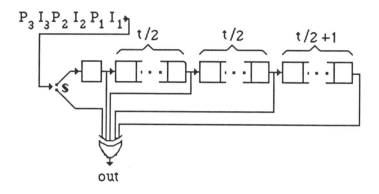

Fig. 6.3 The inverse of the encoder

Fig. 6.2. Here the sequence ...$P_3\,I_3\,P_2\,I_2\,P_1\,I_1$, generated by the encoder, is fed directly (no errors are introduced yet) into the input of the switch S which splits the information bits ... $I_3\,I_2\,I_1$ and the parity bits ... $P_3\,P_2\,P_1$ into separate streams. The information bits are fed to the top channel, entering the shift register. The parity bits enter the bottom channel and are fed into the XOR gate. In clock period #j (where #1 is a reference point in time) the five inputs to the XOR gate are $P_j,\ I_j,\ I_{(j-t/2)},\ I_{(j-t)},\ I_{(j-3t/2-1)}.$ $(I_{(j-t/2)}$ denotes the $(j-t/2)$th information bit.) Observing the encoder of Fig. 6.2, we note that P_j $= I_j + I_{j-t/2} + I_{(j-t)} + I_{(j-3t/2-1)}.$ This means that the output from the XOR gate of Fig. 6.3 is constantly 0 since the input P_j always equals the sum of the other four inputs to the XOR gate. The stream ... $P_3\,I_3\,P_2$ $I_2\,P_1\,I_1$ generated by the encoder is transmitted, but may be subject to

errors. Let its received version be denoted by ... $p_3\,i_3\,p_2\,i_2\,p_1 i_1...$.
When these received bits are fed into a circuit of the form depicted in
Fig. 6.3, the outputs from the XOR gate are not necessarily 0 all
the time.

Let

(1) $p_j = P_j + Y_j$

(2) $i_j = I_j + Z_j$

Bits Y_j and Z_j are the "error indication bits". If $Y_j = 1$, then p_j is
erroneous. If $Z_j = 1$, then i_j is erroneous.

For ... $p_3\,i_3\,p_2\,i_2\,p_1\,i_1$ being the input to the circuit of Fig. 6.3,
the output from the XOR gate when a certain p_j is received is

$$p_j + i_j + i_{j(j-t/2)} + i_{(j-t)} + i_{(j-3t/2-1)}.$$

Based on equations (1) and (2) this output is:

$$\{P_j + Y_j\} + \{I_j + Z_j\} + \{I_{j-t/2} + Z_{j-t/2}\}$$
$$+ \{I_{(j-t)} + Z_{(j-t)}\} + \{I_{(j-3t/2-1)} + Z_{(j-3t/2-1)}\}$$
$$= \{P_j + I_j + I_{j-t/2} + I_{(j-t)} + I_{(j-3t/2-1)}\}$$
$$+ \{Y_j + Z_j + Z_{j-t/2} + Z_{(j-t)} + Z_{(j-3t/2-1)}\}.$$

Note now that the contents of the first parenthesis equals 0, as was already described before. *The output from the XOR gate then equals the contents of the second parenthesis, which is the sum of the corresponding error indication bits.*

When treating block codes, it was shown that the error syndrome obtained by multiplying a received message by the parity matrix equals the result obtained by multiplying only the error pattern by this matrix. The above observation is an identical property for convolutional codes.

From now on the outputs of the XOR gate in Fig. 6.3 will only be expressed in terms of the error indication bits Y_j and Z_j. The decoder of the diffuse threshold-decoding codes is based primarily on the circuit of Fig. 6.3. As shown next, some extra circuitry is added to this basic circuit for the purpose of detecting whether a certain Z_j equals 1. In that case the corresponding informaion bit I_j is detected to be erroneous and is corrected.

The purpose of the decoder will be just to correct information bits. This does not mean that the parity bits are not allowed to be erroneous. We just do not bother to correct them, although we must base the correction scheme on the fact that they might be erroneous. Here we see a distinct difference between the diffuse threshold-decoding code and the codes with which we were concerned up to now. In these codes we treated parity bits and information bits equally, and the decoding scheme corrected *any* received bit in the same manner.

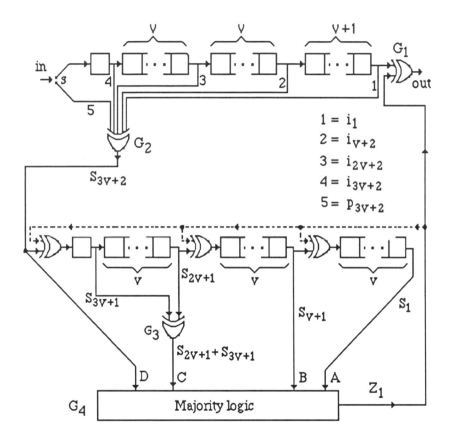

Fig. 6.4   The decoder of the diffuse threshold - decoding convolutional
           codes

The decoder of a diffuse threshold-decoding code is depicted in Fig.
6.4. For ease of notation the value $t/2$ is denoted here by v. The various
values written in various places in the drawing are those obtained
when the bit $p_{(3v+2)}$ is received (it just entered the "in" line at the top left
corner). i_1 denotes here the first received bit. It is the received version

of I_1 which was the bit that started the transmission. (No bits were transmitted before I_1.)

The upper part of the figure is identical to Fig. 6.3, where v denotes t/2. i_1 just exits from the right and enters input #1 of the XOR gate G_2. Input #2 to G_2 is the information bit received v + 1 places after i_1 since, as seen in the figure, there is a delay of v + 1 bits between inputs #1 and #2. The value at input #2 is therefore $i_{(v+2)}$. Input #3 is delayed v bits compared to #2. The value there is therefore $i_{(2v+2)}$. For the same reason input #4 has presently the value $i_{(3v+2)}$. Input #5 has the value $p_{(3v+2)}$, which is the presently received bit. $S_{(3v+2)}$ is the present output from G_2. (Generally, if p_j is the bit received at a certain instant, for some j, then S_j is G_2's output at that instant.)   As was indicated, G_2's output equals the sum of the error indication bits. We then have:

(a) $S_{(3v+2)} = Y_{(3v+2)} + Z_{(3v+2)} + Z_{(2v+2)} + Z_{(v+2)} + Z_1$

The outputs of G_2 enter a register consisting of four sections. The first section is a single stage, and the other three sections are v stages long. The XOR gates inserted between these sections will be treated later. We also disregard momentarily the drawn broken lines.

If the present cycle's output from G_2 is $S_{(3v+2)}$, the output from the subsequent sections of the bottom register are $S_{(3v+1)}, S_{(2v+1)}, S_{(v+1)},$

and S_1, as indicated in the drawing. S_1, which is now fed from the rightmost stage of the register, was the output value of G_2 when p_1 was received. Let us check the five inputs to G_2 during that clock cycle. Input #5 had the value p_1, and #4 had the value i_1 . Since i_1 was the first received bit, the top register is still reset to 0, and inputs #3, 2, 1 all read 0. We then have:

(b) $S_1 = Y_1 + Z_1$.

$S_{(v+1)}$ is the value that was the output of G_2 when $p_{(v+1)}$ was received. At this cycle the value on line #3 is i_1. Input #4 carries the value $i_{(v+1)}$ and #5 carries $p_{(v+1)}$. Lines #1 and #2 still carry 0's. We then have:

(c) $S_{(v+1)} = Y_{(v+1)} + Z_{(v+1)} + Z_1$.

$S_{(2v+1)}$ was generated when $p_{(2v+1)}$ was received. i_1 was then the value at input #2 of G_2. Inputs #3, 4, 5 carried, respectively, the values $i_{(v+1)}, i_{(2v+1)}, p_{(2v+1)}$. We then have:

(d) $S_{(2v+1)} = Y_{(2v+1)} + Z_{(2v+1)} + Z_{(v+1)} + Z_1$.

$S_{(3v+1)}$ was generated when $p_{(3v+1)}$ was received. This is the last time that input #1 to G_2 still carries a 0 by definition. i_1 resides now in the right stage of the top register and will be fed out in the next shift. Inputs #2, 3, 4, 5 carry now, respectively, the values $i_{(v+1)}, i_{(2v+1)},$

$i_{(3v+1)}$ and $p_{(3v+1)}$. We then have:

(e) $S_{(3v+1)} = Y_{(3v+1)} + Z_{(3v+1)} + Z_{(2v+1)} + Z_{(v+1)}$

The output of gate G_3 is:

(f) $S_{(2v+1)} + S_{(3v+1)} = \{Y_{(2v+1)} + Z_{(2v+1)} + Z_{(v+1)} + Z_1\}$

$$+ \{Y_{(3v+1)} + Z_{(3v+1)} + Z_{(2v+1)} + Z_{(v+1)}\}$$

$$= Y_{(3v+1)} + Y_{(2v+1)} + Z_{(3v+1)} + Z_1$$

(Note that $Z_{(2v+1)}$ and $Z_{(v+1)}$ canceled in pairs.)

Gate G_4, named **majority logic**, is a logic gate whose output is 1 if and only if the majority of its inputs are 1. (i.e., if 3 or 4 inputs have value 1). Otherwise, the output is 0.

Based on equations (b), (c), (f), (a), the values at the four inputs to the majority logic gate are (the letters refer to those marked in the figure):

$A = Y_1 + Z_1$

$B = Y_{(v+1)} + Z_{(v+1)} + Z_1$

$C = Y_{(3v+1)} + Y_{(2v+1)} + Z_{(3v+1)} + Z_1$

$D = Y_{(3v+2)} + Z_{(3v+2)} + Z_{(2v+2)} + Z_{(v+2)} + Z_1$

Note now an essential property of A, B, C, D. There are altogether eleven different error -indication bits in the four expressions. Z_1 appears in each expression. Any of the other ten error- indication bits appears only once. This means that if only $Z_1 = 1$, then $A = B = C = D = 1$. If besides Z_1 at most one bit out of the other ten is allowed to be 1, then at least three expressions out of A, B, C, D have a value 1. (The other bit with value 1 will be canceled together with Z_1, making the expression where they both appear to be 0. Z_1 is still the only one appearing in any of the other three expressions having a value 1.)

We next explain how an error burst of length t = 2v, starting with Z_1, ensures that a majority of A, B, C, D has a value 1. Fig. 6.5 demonstrates the distribution of the eleven error- indication bits which appear in A, B, C, D. It shows which bits appear successively and the size of the gaps between bits that do not appear successively. Assume that a burst error of length t = 2v occurred in the received bits, starting with the first received bit i_1. We further assume that this burst error is followed by a recovery region consisting of at least 4v + 4 bits. If the burst error starts with i_1, this means that $Z_1 = 1$. Observing Fig. 6.5, we see that out of the eleven error-indication bits, the only other bit beside Z_1 that falls within

$$Y_{3v+2} \, Z_{3v+2} \, Y_{3v+1} \, Z_{3v+1} \, \cdots \, \underbrace{Z_{2v+2} \, Y_{2v+1}}_{2v\text{-}3} \, \cdots \, \underbrace{Z_{v+2} \, Y_{v+1}}_{2v\text{-}2} \, Z_{v+1} \, \cdots \, \underbrace{Y_1 \, Z_1}_{2v\text{-}2}$$

Fig. 6.5 The distribution of the error indication bits in A,B,C,D

the burst is Y_1. The rest of the bits fall in the recovery region and are 0 by definition. In order for these bits to be 0, it is sufficient that the size of the recovery region be $4v + 4$. The effect of the burst error on the value of A, B, C, D is now clear. If only $Z_1 = 1$, then $A = B = C = D = 1$. The only other possibility is $Z_1 = Y_1 = 1$ in which case $A = 0$, $B = C = D = 1$.

Conclusion 6.1   If an error burst of length $t = 2v$ occurs in the reccived bits, starting with i_1 and followed by a recovery region of size $4v + 4$, then the output of G_4 is 1. If i_1 is error free then the output of G_4 is 0. In other words *The output of G_4 is Z_1.*

As seen in Fig. 6.4, the output of G_4 is XORed with i_1 before the final output is generated.   Since this output is Z_1, it follows that the final output of the decoder, fed out of G_1, is $i_1 + Z_1 = I_1$. The originally transmitted bit I_1 is thus recovered.

In the preceding discussion, i_1 was specifically the received version of the first *transmitted* bit. The entire discussion is, however, still valid if i_1 is considered to be the first *erroneous* information bit that was received. This is due to the fact that so long as there are no errors, the contents of the bottom register (containing the S_j's) are "all 0", and all the considerations in the above explantion are unchanged. (It is left to the reader, as an exercise, to figure out what happens if the first received erroneous bit is an originally transmitted parity bit.)

We have just shown how the first bit out of an error burst of length t = 2v is corrected. We have not shown why the entire burst is corrected. The explanation is straightforward. Equations (a), (b), (c), (d), (e), (f) are still valid if we add 1 to all the indexes. The reasoning behind the fact that the output of G_1 is Z_1 (for the values displayed in Fig. 6.4) is valid for $Z_2, Z_3, ... ,Z_v$. The first v outputs of G_1 are therefore the original v information bits. Since there is a parity bit between any two information bits, the correction of v successive information bits is equivalent to the correction of burst error of length 2v occurring in the transmitted bits. This reasoning also explains the necessity of having a recovery region of length 6v + 2, since by adding v − 1 to each of the indexes in Fig. 6.5 (yielding a first bit with index v), the last bit is Y_{4v+1}. The last bit of the corrected burst is Y_v. There is a distance of 6v + 2 transmitted bits between Y_v and Y_{4v+1}, and all the bits within this range must be error free in order for the scheme to work. (We already explained before why all the bits between $Z_{(v+1)}$ and $Y_{(3v+2)}$ must be error free in order for G_4 to produce Z_1. Now we add v − 1 to all these indexes.)

The preceding explanation clarified how a burst error of length 2v is corrected, based on the existence of a recovery region whose length is *at least* 6v+2. The words "at least" are based on the fact that a shorter recovery region will invalidate the scheme. The question is whether a recovery region of size $6v+2$ is *sufficient* for a further correct functioning of the scheme. In other words, if we have another erroneous bit i_j following immediately the $6v+2$ error-free bits, can we correct it by simply shifting on the circuit of Fig. 6.4? In order to correct i_j, we need that the bottom register (containing the S_j's) will be reset when i_j enters. If this condition is satisfied, then for all practical purposes i_j can be treated in the same way as i_1 was treated before. This is enabled by the drawn broken line and the XOR gates spread along the bottom register, depicted in Fig. 6.4. The purpose of this circuitry is to reset this register if $6v+2$ error free bits follow a burst error. The resetting is clarified by observing equations (a), (c), (d). Each $S_{(3v+2)}$, $S_{(2v+1)}$ and $S_{(v+1)}$, stored in the bottom register, contains Z_1 as one of its addends. Note that Z_1 is fed through the broken line and XORed with $S_{(3v+2)}$, $S_{(2v+1)}$ and $S_{(v+1)}$. Z_1 then cancels itself in equations (a), (c), (d). By the same token the other addends in these equations also cancel themselves, upon their generation, by G_4. The register is then guaranteed to be reset at the right time, enabling the correction of further burst errors.

APPENDIX
THE BASIC PRINCIPLES RE-EXAMINED

A.1 Polynomial Division Modulo 2

The limited mathematics used until now included varied elementary operations from linear algebra and a trace of modular arithmetic. These enabled us to get quite far. Complete encoding and decoding processes were entirely understood. In this appendix we review mathematical tools especially suitable for error correction design and analysis. The basic principles presented in the preceding chapters will be re-examined, using these tools, to demonstrate their power.

First, we consider the polynomial division modulo 2 operation. Here all polynomials have binary coefficients. Addition operations involved in the division are executed modulo 2 (i.e., a+a = 0). In other words, as before, addition is our standard XOR operation and addition is identical to subtraction.

Let us demonstrate how two polynomials are divided:

$$x^6 + x^5 + x^3 + x^2 + 1 \quad : \quad x^3 + x + 1 =$$
$$\text{dividend} \qquad\qquad \text{divisor}$$

At each step of the division operation we divide the term with the highest exponent in the dividend, by the term with the highest exponent in the divisor, and write the result as a term of the quotient. We then multiply this term of the quotient by the entire divisor and add the result to the dividend. For example, consider the above sample dividend and divisor.

Presently, the term with the highest exponent in the dividend is x^6. The term with the highcst exponent in the divisor is x^3. Dividing x^6 by x^3 yields x^3, that is the first term of the quotient. Multiplying x^3 by $x^3 + x + 1$ yields $x^6 + x^4 + x^3$. Adding now this result to the dividend yields $x^5 + x^4 + x^2 + 1$. The described process is written technically as:

$$x^6 + x^5 + x^3 + x^2 + 1 \quad : \quad x^3 + x + 1 = x^3$$
$$\underline{x^6 + x^4 + x^3}$$
$$x^5 + x^4 + x^2 + 1$$

We apply now the same process to the polynomial $x^5 + x^4 + x^2 + 1$; that is, we divide x^5 (that is presently the term with the highest exponent) by x^3 and get x^2. The next term of the quotient is therefore x^2. We then multiply x^2 by $x^3 + x + 1$ and get $x^5 + x^3 + x^2$, that is addcd to $x^5 + x^4 + x^2 + 1$. The entire division operation is then executed as follows:

$$
\begin{array}{l}
x^6 + x^5 + x^3 + x^2 + 1 \; : \; x^3 + x + 1 = x^3 + x^2 + x + 1 \\
\underline{x^6 + x^4 + x^3} \hspace{4.5cm} \text{quotient} \\
\quad\; x^5 + x^4 + x^2 + 1 \\
\quad\; \underline{x^5 + x^3 + x^2} \\
\qquad\quad x^4 + x^3 + 1 \\
\qquad\quad \underline{x^4 + x^2 + x} \\
\qquad\qquad\;\; x^3 + x^2 + x + 1 \\
\qquad\qquad\;\; \underline{x^3 + x + 1} \\
\qquad\qquad\qquad x^2 \quad \text{remainder}
\end{array}
$$

The process terminates when the remainder is a polynomial whose degree is of lower order than that of the divisor. Here our remainder is x^2. The remainder can, of course, be 0. This happens when the dividend is a multiple of the divisor.

Since our polynomials all have binary coefficients, they can be written as binary vectors, representing only the coefficients of the polynomials. For example, the polynomial $x^6 + x^5 + x^3 + x^2 + 1 = 1 \cdot x^6 + 1 \cdot x^5 + 0 \cdot x^4 + 1 \cdot x^3 + 1 \cdot x^2 + 0 \cdot x^1 + 1 \cdot x^0$ is represented by 1101101, a seven bits long vector. The bit in place #i, counting from the right, is the value of the coefficient of x^i, where the first place is #0. The polynomial $x^3 + x + 1$ is presented as 1011.

The preceding division then has the following binary presentation:

```
1101101  :  1011 = 1111
1011
 110101
 1011
  11001
  1011
   1111
   1011
    100
```

A.2 The Connection between Polynomial Division and LFSR Circuitry

As will be shown later, an operation that is of a great practical need is the calculation of $f(x) \bmod g(x)$, that is, calculating the remainder obtained after dividing the polynomial f(x) by g(x). (The division operation is always of the binary form treated in section A.1.)

Let us turn again to the operation demonstrated in the preceding section. (The operation 1101101 : 1011.) As observed there, that operation can be described as follows. In the first step, we put the vector 1011 under the dividend, where the left most 1 of 1011 falls under the 1 on the left of 1101101. Adding the two vectors then decreases the degree of the dividend by one. We do now the same operation on the vector 110101, derived from the previous step. That is, we move the divisor until the leftmost 1's of 1011 and 110101 coincide, thereby further decreasing the degree of the previous polynomial. This operation is repeated until the final remainder is a polynomial of degree 2 or less (i.e., a binary vector of length 3).

The above process can be described differently. Take the polynomial 1101101, cancel its leftmost 1 and invert the two bits that are two and three places to the right of this 1. Do the same operation on the resultant vector etc. (i.e., on each vector cancel the leftmost 1 and invert the bits that are two and three places on its right). This process can be implemented in hardware using the circuit depicted in Fig. A.1.

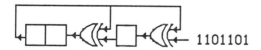 1101101

Fig. A.1 A circuit for calculating $(x^6 + x^5 + x^3 + x^2 + 1)$ mod $(x^3 + x + 1)$

The coefficients of the dividend are fed into a linear feedback shift register that is initially reset (all registers read zero). When a 1 leaves the left stage it "falls out" while adding a 1 to the bits that are two and three places to the right. This is exactly what is done in the division operation described above. The final contents of the register (after the entire dividend is shifted in) is the required remainder.

The specific dividend $x^6 + x^5 + x^3 + x^2 + 1$ treated in the above example can be replaced by any general polynomial g(x). The circuit of Fig. A.1 is then a general circuit generating g(x) mod $(x^3 + x + 1)$.

A revealing observation would be that *the circuit of Fig. A.1 is identical to the syndrome generator depicted in Fig. 3.2 (redrawn in Fig. A.2).* One circuit is actually a reflection of the other. They are, of course, still identical since a circuit will not change its functioning if one will turn over the page on which the circuit is drawn.

From now on we stick to conventional drawing, as depicted in Fig A.2, where the input is fed from the left. In order to formulize the demonstrated identity between the two figures, we need the following definitions.

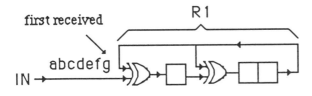

Fig. A.2   Fig. 3.2 redrawn

Definition **The polynomial corresponding to a vector M or the polynomial represented by M** refers to the polynomial whose coefficients are the bits of M.   **We denote this polynomial by M(x).**

Example The polynomial corresponding to the vector M = (1001011) is $M(x) = 1 + x^3 + x^5 + x^6$. (Note that the rightmost bit of M is the coefficient of the highest exponent. This ordering will be consistent, unless otherwise specified.)

Definition   (Clarifying details will follow.)
1. **The polynomial corresponding to a LFSR** is a polynomial whose coefficients correspond to the feedback connections of the LFSR.
2. **The LFSR corresponding to a polynomial** is the LFSR whose feedback connections correspond to the coefficients of the polynomial.
If R denotes the LFSR, then R(x) denotes its corresponding polynomial, and vice versa.

The connection between polynomials and their corresponding LFSR's can be explained as follows: it is first required that the number of stages of the LFSR should equal the degree of the polynomial. Mark the stages of the LFSR, starting from the left, by successive powers of x, starting with 0. The rightmost stage will then be marked by x^{n-1}, where n is the degree of the polynomial. *The feedback line, originating from the rightmost stage, is fed back to all the stages marked by the powers of x that appear in the polynomial.* This connection enables us to recover a corresponding LFSR from a given polynomial. The process of recovering the polynomial corresponding to a given LFSR is similar. The nonzero coefficients of the polynomial correspond to those stages of the LFSR that are connected to the feedback line. If n is the length of the LFSR, the coefficient of x^n in the polynomial is 1.

Example

1. Observe the connection between the polynomial $1 + x + x^3$ and the LFSR of Fig. 3.2 or 3.1.

2. Take the three LFSR's depicted in Fig. 5.8 redrawn in Fig. A.3.

The polynomials corresponding to these LFSR's are

(a) CRC-12: $f(x) = x^{12} + x^{11} + x^3 + x^2 + x + 1$;

(b) CRC-16: $f(x) = x^{16} + x^{15} + x^2 + 1$;

(c) CRC-CCITT: $f(x) = x^{16} + x^{12} + x^5 + 1$

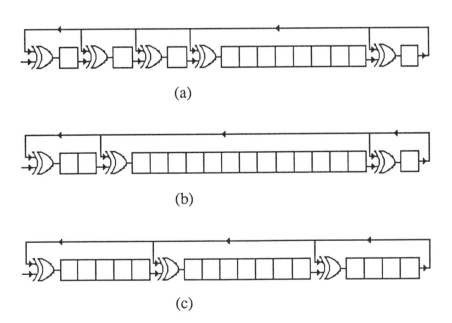

(a)

(b)

(c)

Fig. A.3   Fig. 5.8 redrawn

The observation made at the beginning of this section, concerning the identity betwcen Fig. A.1 and Fig. A.2, can now be stated formally.

Proposition A.1   Let R be an LFSR. Let C denote the contents of R obtained after shifting a vector V into it. Then $C(x) = V(x) \bmod R(x)$. (In other words, the contents of R, obtained after shifting V into it, forms the coefficients of the remainder obtained by dividing the polynomial corresponding to V by the polynomial corresponding to R.)

We do not give the proof of Proposition A.1 in a formal manner. The detailed demonstration given before clearly validates the proposition.

It is important to note that Proposition A.1 actually means that **an LFSR connected in the form depicted in Fig. A.2 or Fig. A.3 is in practice a division circuit,** dividing the polynomial shifted into it by the polynomial represented by the feedback connections of the LFSR. The final contents of the LFSR is the remainder of the division operation.

By observing the functioning of the circuit of Fig. A.1, it can be easily verified that the successive contents of the leftmost stage of the LFSR form the coefficients of the *quotient* of the division operation. (In the circuits of Figs. A.2 or A.3 the quotient is generated by the rightmost stage.) However, in the implementations relevant to error-correcting codes there is no practical need for the quotient.

Next we interpret the behavior of a free-running LFSR from the

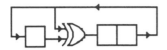

Fig. A.4   Fig. 3.1   redrawn

polynomial perspective. Such an LFSR is depicted in Fig. 3.1 redrawn in
Fig. A.4.

Proposition A.2   Let R be a free-running LFSR. Its contents after the
i-th shift, starting with the initial contents (1000 ... 0), is the polynomial
representation of x^i mod R(x).

Shift #	*Binary Contents*	*Polynomial Representation*	
0	1 0 0	1	$= x^0$ mod R(x)
1	0 1 0	x^1	$= x^1$ mod R(x)
2	0 0 1	x^2	$= x^2$ mod R(x)
3	1 1 0	$1 + x$	$= x^3$ mod R(x)
4	0 1 1	$x + x^2$	$= x^4$ mod R(x)
5	1 1 1	$1 + x + x^2$	$= x^5$ mod R(x)
6	1 0 1	$1 + x^2$	$= x^6$ mod R(x)
7	1 0 0	1	$= x^7$ mod R(x)
etc			

Table A.1   Successive contents of the register of Fig.A.4
            ($R(x) = 1 + x + x^3$)

Example Table A.1 lists the successive contents of the register of Fig A.4, and their corresponding polynomials.

Proof of Proposition A.2 For tutorial purposes we give two intuitive variations of the proof.

Variation 1

The initial contents 100 ... 0 correspond to the polynomial x^0. Generally, the polynomial $x \cdot f(x)$ is obtained by shifting all the coefficients of $f(x)$ for one place to the right. After the first $n - 1$ shifts, when the 1 element gets to the n-th stage, the contents of the register correspond to x^{n-1}. After an additional shift, which is a further multiplication by x, the contents of the register correspond to x^n. What actually happens is that the register will have 1's in all the stages connected to the feedback line. We claim that these contents correspond to the polynomial $x^n \bmod R(x)$, based on the following observation. R(x) is of degree n. Taking x^n modulo R(x) yields as a result a polynomial that is obtained by dropping the term x^n from R(x). (For example, $x^3 \bmod (1 + x + x^3) = 1 + x$.) Our feedback connections are then exactly made such that shifting the contents x^{n-1} once more, yields the contents $x^n \bmod R(x)$. This explains why successive shifts of the register generate successive powers of x modulo R(x).

We explain this further, using an example. Consider the register of Fig. A.4, whose feedback connections correspond to the polynomial R(x) $= 1 + x + x^3$. We know that $x^3 \bmod (1 + x + x^3) = 1 + x$. Observe now the successive contents of the register, listed in Table A.1. Following the contents 001, the rightmost 1 is shifted out and is replaced by $1 + x = x^3$

mod $(1 + x + x^3)$. Each additional shift of the register multiplies the contents by x, therefore generating successive powers of x, where x^3 is always replaced by x^3 mod R(x). That is, the powers of x are generated mod R(x).

Variation 2

This variation of the proof of Proposition A.2 is based on the connection between a free-running LFSR, of the form depicted in Fig. A.4, and the division circuit, of the form depicted in Fig A.2. The proof, which is based on Proposition A.1, treats specifically these two LFSR's. Its generality will then be obvious.

For simplicity the register of Fig. A.4 is denoted here by R, whereas that of of Fig A.2 is denoted by R1. We first claim that the contents of R after i shifts, starting with the initial state (100), is equivalent to the final contents of R1, obtained after shifting into it a vector Vi of length 7, having a single 1 element in place #i, counting from the left. (The first place on the left is #0.) In order to understand why, observe that the initial contents of R1 is "all 0". The contents will remain "all 0" during the first 6-i shifts, after which a 1 is shifted in. The contents of R1 is then (100). This register will now run free like the register R for additional i shifts, until the rest of Vi is shifted in. Its final contents is then the contents of R after i shifts, starting with the initial state (100).

Example Shift the vector V4 = (0000100) into R1. For the first 2 shifts R1 will still contain "all 0". A 1 is then shifted in, and the circuit continue to shift four more times. The final contents of R1 is then (011), that is the contents of R after four shifts, starting with the initial state (100).

Continuing the proof, we apply now Proposition A.1. The polynomial representation of Vi is $Vi(x) = x^i$. We then have that the contents of R after i shifts, starting with the initial state (100), represents the polynomial $x^i \bmod (1 + x + x^3)$. This completes the proof of Proposition A.2.

Note that it was shown in chapter 3 that the free-running LFSR of Fig A.4 generates the rows of the martix H'. Proposition A.2 then means that *the i-th row of H' represents the polynomial $x^i \bmod R(x)$*, where $R(x) = (1 + x + x^3)$. We claim that for B being a vector of length 7, the product B·H' yields the polynomial $B(x) \bmod R(x)$. This can be shown as follows: For B= (abcdefg),

$$B \cdot H' = a[x^0 \bmod R(x)] + b[x^1 \bmod R(x)] + c[x^2 \bmod R(x)] +$$
$$d[x^3 \bmod R(x)] + e[x^4 \bmod R(x)] + f[x^5 \bmod R(x)] +$$
$$g[x^6 \bmod R(x)]$$

Based on a known basic identity, the right side of the above equation equals:
$$[a + bx + cx^2 + dx^3 + ex^4 + fx^5 + gx^6] \bmod R(x)$$
$$= B(x) \bmod R(x).$$

The fact that B·H' yields the polynomial $B(x) \bmod R(x)$ is not surprising, since we know that Fig. A.2 is on the one hand, a division circuit and, on the other, a circuit that performs a vector-matrix multiplication (as shown in chapter 3). The considerations related to the matrix H' were therefore, in a sense, a repetition of Propositions A.1 and

A.2. They were brought here, however, to illuminate the issue from a further angle.

A.3 *The Generating Polynomial of a Code*

A.3.1 *Re-Examining Some Basic Properties of a Cyclic Code*

As defined in chapter 4, a cyclic code is any code generated by an LFSR. (We also explained there that not every such code actually has the cyclic property, in the sense that a cyclic shift of a code word is also a code word, unless the length of a code word is Pu.) From now on we refer only to such codes. Based on Proposition A.1 we have the following *major* conclusion.

Conclusion A.1 Let M be a transmitted code word of a cyclic code. M' is the received version of M. Let R denote the generating LFSR of the code, and let S denote the error syndrome obtained by shifting M' into R. Then $S(x) = M'(x) \bmod R(x)$.

Proposition A.3 Let C be a cyclic code generated by register R, where the length of a code word is n. Then the vector V of length n is a code word of C if and only if $V(x)$ is a multiple of $R(x)$.

Example Consider the (7, 4) code generated by the LFSR of Fig. A.2. Here $R(x) = (1 + x + x^3)$. The vector V = (1110010) is a code word of our code since the polynomial $V(x) = 1 + x + x^2 + x^5$, corresponding to V, is divisible by $R(x)$. On the other hand, the vector W = (1111000) is not a code word of our code since the polynomial $W(x) = 1 + x + x^2 + x^3$ is not divisible by $R(x)$.

Proof of Proposition A.3 We know from chapter 3 that V is a code word of C if and only if the error syndrome obtained by shifting V into R is "all 0". From Conclusion A.1 we know that an "all 0" syndrome is equivalent mathematically to the equation $V(x) \bmod R(x) = 0$. (The 0 on the right hand side of the equation is the *polynomial* 0, i.e., a polynomial whose coefficients are all 0.) This equation means that when dividing $V(x)$ by $R(x)$ the remainder is 0. That is, $V(x)$ is a multiple of $R(x)$. This completes the proof of the proposition.

For convenience we shall not distinguish between a vector V and the polynomial $V(x)$ from now on. A sentence like "$f(x)$ is a code word of **C**" is absolutely legitimate (where we actually mean the *vector* f corresponding to $f(x)$ is a code word of **C**).

Conclusion A.2 Let **C** be an (n, k) cyclic code generated by register R of length $n - k$. The code words of C are all the polynomials of degree n-1 or less, that are a multiple of $R(x)$. (The degree of $R(x)$ is the length of the generating LFSR of the code. This is also the number of parity bits.) In order to check whether a received message is still a valid code word, what the receiver is actually doing is checking whether or not the received message, when being treated as a polynomial, is still divisible by $R(x)$.

Definition Let **C** be a cyclic code whose code words are all the polynomials of degree n-1 or less, that are divisible by a polynomial $R(x)$. $R(x)$ is called **the generating polynomial of the code**.

Having introduced polynomial arithmetic as a basic tool for handling cyclic codes, let us review Proposition 4.1 that is re-stated next.

Proposition 4.1   Let C be an (n, k) code whose parity matrix is the matrix M, and let G denote the generating matrix of C. (The rows of M are generated by successive shifts of an LFSR of length q, starting with the initial state (1000 ... 0)).)

1. Any code word of C consists of the sum of some linear shifts to the right of the first row of G, where the shifts are of no more than $k - 1$ places.

2. Any vector of length n that consists of the sum of some linear shifts to the right of the first row of G, where the shifts are for no more than k-1 places, must be a code word of C.

As was already clarified there, $q = n-k$. The first q bits in the first row of G denote the feedback connections of the generating LFSR, the (q+1)-th bit is 1, and the rest of the bits are 0. Based on the experience we have already gained in this chapter, it is clear that the first q+1 bits in the first row of G are the coefficients of the generating polynomial R(x) of the code, whose degree is $n - k$, where a linear shift by i places to the right of this row yields the polynomial $x^i \cdot R(x)$. Proposition 4.1 then means that V(x) is a code word of C if and only if V(x) is of the form

$A0 \cdot R(x) + A1 \cdot x \cdot R(x) + A2 \cdot x^2 \cdot R(x) + \cdots + A(K-1) \cdot x^{k-1} \cdot R(x)$.

Proposition 4.1 then means that V(x) is a code word of C if and only if $V(x) = R(x) \cdot (A0 + A1 \cdot x + A2 \cdot x^2 + \cdots + A(K-1) \cdot x^{k-1})$. Note now that this last expression is the general form of any polynomial of degree n-1 or less that is a multiple of R(x). (The degree is $n - 1$ or less since R(x) is of degree $n - k$. Multiplying it by a polynomial of degree $k - 1$ or less yields a polynomial of degree $n - 1$ or less.) We then have that *Proposition 4.1 is identical to Conclusion A.2.*

A.3.2 Re-Examining the Decoding Procedure of a Cyclic Code in General, and Single Error Correction Hamming Code in Particular.

We now consider the polynomial arithmetic aspects of the decoding procedure of a cyclic code. The transmitted code word $V(x)$ of such a code is characterized by the fact that it is divisible by a certain generating polynomial $R(x)$. Upon receiving the message $V'(x)$, the decoding process at the receiver starts by checking whether $V'(x)$ is still divisible by $R(x)$. This is done by shifting $V'(x)$ into a division circuit. This operation yields the error syndrome polynomial $S(x) = V'(x) \bmod R(x)$. The coefficients of $S(x)$ are therefore all 0 if and only if $V'(x)$ is divisible by $R(x)$. In this case it is determined that $V'(x)$ is a valid code word. If $S(x)$ has at least one nonzero coefficient, it is detected that $V'(x)$ is an erroneous message.

Let us now see in some detail the single error-correction procedure of a Hamming code. If the received message $V'(x)$ differs from the transmitted message $V(x)$ in coefficient #j, and only there, then $V'(x) = V(x) + x^j$. We then have that:

$$S(x) = V'(x) \bmod R(x) = (V(x) + x^j) \bmod R(x) = V(x) \bmod R(x) + x^j \bmod R(x).$$

Since $V(x) \bmod R(x) = 0$, we have that:

$$S(x) = x^j \bmod R(x).$$

In order to find the error location j, a circuit of the form depicted in Figs. 3.4 or 3.7b generates successive powers of x modulo $R(x)$, starting with

x^j, until the value of x^0 is detected. Since $x^0 = x^{(2^n-1)}$, it follows that the number of shifts is 2^n-1-j, that enables the recovery of the value of j.

A.3.3 The Encoding Process Re-Examined

The encoding process of cyclic codes was described in chapter 3. Here we give it a more formal treatment using polynomial arithmetic. If R(x) is the generating polynomial of the code, the encoding process will be to convert an information polynomial I(x) of degree k-1 or less (corresponding to the information vector I of length k), into a code word V(x) divisible by R(x). An obvious way of obtaining such a V(x) is simply to multiply I(x) by R(x). This, however, will not yield a systematic code (in which k – 1 successive coefficients of V(x) should consist of the coefficients of I(x)). The encoding process depicted in Fig. 3.3, redrawn in Fig. A.5, generates a V(x) of a systematic code. We now review this process in terms of polynomial manipulations.

Let us first see a connection between the operation of the circuits of Figs. A.2 and A.5. We claim that the contents of R1 of Fig. A.2, obtained by shifting the vector (000abcd) into it, is identical to the contents of the LFSR of Fig.A.5, obtained by shifting (abcd) into it. This can be verified by a direct check, showing that the final contents in both cases is (a+c+d, a+b+c, b+c+d). The logic behind this identity follows

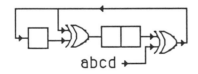

Fig. A.5   Fig. 3.3 redrawn

from observing that in the first case the first three shifts push d to the right stage. The operation of this circuit for the next four shifts, is now identical to the operation of the second circuit, starting with the first shift, since the second circuit *starts* operating at the step where d is already shifted out of the right stage of the LFSR.

Next we analyze the operation of the encoder of Fig. A.5 in terms of shifting the vector (000abcd) into the division circuit of Fig. A.2. The information vector represents the polynomial $I(x) = a + bx + cx^2 + dx^3$. The vector $J = (000abcd)$ represents the polynomial $J(x) = ax^3 + bx^4 + cx^5 + dx^6$. The contents of R1 after $J(x)$ is shifted into it are $P(x) = J(x)$ mod $(1 + x + x^3)$. The polynomial $J(x) + P(x)$ is therefore divisible by $x^3 + x + 1$. (If you subtract from a value A the value of A mod B, the result is divisible by B. Here we add since in a XOR operation addition and subtraction are identical.) As the degree of $P(x)$ is 2 or less, adding $P(x)$ to $J(x)$ is equivalent to the replacement of the three 0's at the tail of J by the contents of R1. Going back to the encoder of Fig. A.5, we have then shown that by attaching the contents of the LFSR (after abcd is shifted into it) to abcd, we generate a polynomial that is divisible by $(1 + x + x^3)$, and that has in it the four successive coefficients abcd, that is needed in order for the code to be systematic.

A.4   Cyclic Properties of Polynomials

A.4.1   The Periodicity of an LFSR as Reflected in the Polynomial Corresponding to It

Let an LFSR be shifted starting with the initial contents X. Its periodicity related to the initial contents (1000 ... 0) was denoted by Pu. A maximal periodicity LFSR has the property that when loaded with any nonzero initial value, it passes through all the possible $2^n - 1$ nonzero combinations before returning to the initial setting, that is, for a maximal periodicity LFSR of length n, $Pu = 2^n - 1$. Note that the code generated by a maximal periodicity LFSR is Hamming code.

Let $R(x)$ be the polynomial of degree n corresponding to a register R. In terms of polynomial considerations we say that the register generates polynomials of degree $n - 1$ or less, that are successive powers of x modulo $R(x)$. The polynomials between $x^0 \bmod R(x)$ and $x^{Pu-1} \bmod R(x)$ all have distinct forms, where $x^{Pu} \bmod R(x) = x^0 \bmod R(x)$. *Operations in the exponent are therefore performed modulo Pu.*

Proposition A.4 $(1 + x^{Pu})$ is divisible by $R(x)$

Proof $(1 + x^{Pu}) \bmod R(x) = [1 \bmod R(x)] + [x^{Pu} \bmod R(x)]$. But $x^{Pu} \bmod R(x) = 1$ by definition. Therefore $(1 + x^{Pu}) \bmod R(x) = 1 + 1 = 0$. Obtaining a remainder 0 after dividing $(1 + x^{Pu})$ by $R(x)$ means that $(1 + x^{Pu})$ is divisible by $R(x)$.

Q.E.D.

A.4.2 Why Do We Call Our Codes 'Cyclic'? A Formal Treatment

Proposition 4.1 stated that any code generated by a LFSR, and whose code words are of length Pu, has the cyclic property. That is, a cyclic shift of a code word is also a code word. (As was previously stated, it is customary to give the name "cyclic code" to any code generated by a LFSR, although not all these codes have necessarily the cyclic property.)

We now prove this proposition using the newly introduced mathematical tools.

Step1: **The calculation of f(x) mod (1 + x^n).**

Let us consider what happens when we calculate the value of f(x) mod (1 + x^n), where f(x) is a polynomial of degree > n. For example, calculate $(x^5 + x^3 + x^2 + x + 1)$ mod $(x^3 + 1)$. Momentarily we write here the polynomials in a form where the highest exponent is on the left. This is done in order to be consistent with the division operation that follows:

```
101111  : 1001 = 11
1001
 01011
 1001
  010      remainder = x
```

As already done in section A.1, the division by $x^3 + 1$ means "sliding" the divisor 1001 across the dividend 101111, from left to right. Whenever the 1 on the left of the divisor coincides with a 1 in the dividend, they both cancel, and a 1 is added to the dividend three places to the right of the canceled 1. Note that in the specific case where the divisor is 1001, the above operation is equivalent to "slicing" the dividend 101111 into two halves, namely, 101 and 111, and adding them. That is, 101 + 111 = 010. It can be simply verified that such a "slicing" operation is applicable to all the cases where the only non zero coefficients of the divisor are the ones with the highest and lowest exponent. When the high exponent scans one slice, the low exponent scans the corresponding bits in the slice on the right.

Returning now to the convention where the highest exponent is written on the right, the calculation of $f(x) \bmod (1 + x^n)$ can then be characterized as follows. "Slice" the binary vector representing $f(x)$ into sections that are n bits long, starting from the left. (If the length of the vector is not a multiple of n, attach some 0's to the right of the vector.) Then add these sections one to the other. The result is $f(x) \bmod (1 + x^n)$. This argument is clarified by an example. (1011010111) mod (10001) is calculated as follows: slice the dividend into 4-bit sections. (The divisor is $1 + x^4$). We get 1011, 0101, 1100. (Two 0's were attached on the right of the dividend to make the right section 4 bits long.) Add the three sections:

```
1011
0101
1100
0010
```

The remainder is x^2.

Step 2: **The polynomial representation of two different cyclic shifts of a vector.**

Consider now the connection between a polynomial $f(x)$ that corresponds to a binary vector f of length n, and a polynomial $f^i(x)$ that corresponds to a vector f^i obtained by shifting f cyclically i places to the right. (The degree of either polynomial was not specified. It cannot exceed $n - 1$ but may be less as there can be rightmost 0's in either f or f^i.) The connection between the two polynomials is found as follows. Multiply $f(x)$ by x^i. This will move all the coefficients of $f(x)$ to the right (not cyclically) for i places. $[x^i \cdot f(x)] \bmod (1 + x^n)$ is then the polynomial $f^i(x)$ since, based on what we said before, the modulo operation will add the i coefficients on the right of $x^i f(x)$ to the i 0's that are on its left, which is equivalent to a cyclic shift.

Step 3: **Conclusion**.

Let the code words of a code **C** be of length Pu. We now show that if b is a code word of **C,** then b^i, that is obtained from b by i shifts to the right, is also a code word of **C**. Let R(x) be the generating polynomial of **C**. Then b(x) mod R(x) = 0. The polynomial corresponding to b^i is $b^i(x)$ = $[x^i$ b(x)] mod $(1 + x^{Pu})$, since Pu is the length of both b and b^i.

In order to show that b^i is a code word, we have to show that $[x^i$ b(x)] mod $(1 + x^{Pu})$ is divisible by R(x). This is done next. Note that if b(x) is divisible by R(x), so is x^i b(x). From Proposition A.4 the polynomial $(1 + x^{Pu})$ is also divisible by R(x). It follows that $[x^i$ b(x)] mod $(1 + x^{Pu})$ is also divisible by R(x). (Try a numerical example: 700 is divisible by 7, 21 is also divisible by 7. It then follows that 700 mod 21 is divisible by 7 as well). This completes the new proof of Proposition 4.1.

A.5   More Properties of Cyclic Codes Based on Polynomial Manipulations

A.5.1   The Code Whose Syndrome Decoder Consists of a Parallel Connection of Several LFSR's

We turn now to the issue treated in section 4.4. The decoder of Fig. 4.2, redrawn in Fig. A.6, generated two independent syndromes out of a received message.

The problem that we faced there was to find a single LFSR that generates the same code. We next show how this problem is solved using polynomial arithmetic.

The feedback connections of the two syndrome generators of Fig. A.6

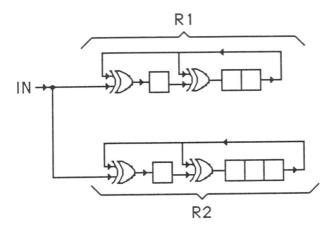

Fig. A.6   Fig. 4.2   redrawn

correspond to the polynomials $(1 + x + x^3)$ and $(1 + x + x^4)$. Since a code word V of our code should yield 0 for both syndromes, we require that $V(x)$ should be divisible by $(1 + x + x^3)$ and by $(1 + x + x^4)$. One way to achieve that is to require that the generating polynomial $R(x)$ of the code be the product of the two polynomials. That is, $R(x) = (1 + x + x^3) \cdot (1 + x + x^4) = (1 + x^2 + x^3 + x^5 + x^7)$. As $V(x)$ is a multiple of $R(x)$, for every code word V, the above form for $R(x)$ will guarantee that $V(x)$ is divisible by $(1 + x + x^3)$ and by $(1 + x + x^4)$.

Note now that $R(x)$ *is exactly the generating polynomial corresponding to the LFSR depicted in Fig. 4.3.* We now quote the process given in section 4.4 for recovering the LFSR that acts like two LFSR's connected in parallel. "The feedback connections of our LFSR are found from multiplying a vector **v** by a matrix **M**, where **v** represents the feedback connections of one register, and the rows of **M** consist of linear shifts of the vector representing the feedback connections of the other register." *It* *is easily verified that this process is identical to multiplying the polynomials corresponding to the two individual LFSR's.* (Readers more familiar with the subject will recognize that the quoted process describes a convolution operation, which, by definition, means in our case a polynomial multiplication.)

Next we relate to the specific case of the decoder of Fig. 5.3. It consists of two individual syndrome decoders connected in parallel, corresponding to the polynomials $(1 + x^5)$ and $(1 + x^3)$. Two possible LFSR's were presented in section 5.9, each one acting as a possible generating LFSR of the code. The register of Fig. 5.4 corresponds to the generating polynomial $(1 + x^3 + x^5 + x^8)$ that equals to the product of the two individual polynomials, and it was obtained by applying the process quoted above. The register of Fig. 5.5 corresponds to the polynomial $(1 + x + x^2 + x^5 + x^6 + x^7)$. It was not explained there how we arrived at this result. This is done now.

The only requirement that the generating polynomial $R(x)$ of our code should satisfy is that it must be divisible by both $(1 + x^5)$ and $(1 + x^3)$. One way of obtaining this is by satisfying the condition $R(x) = (1 + x^5)\cdot(1 + x^3)$. This is, however, only a sufficient condition enabling the divisibility of $R(x)$ by $(1 + x^5)$ and by $(1 + x^3)$. It is actually sufficient that $R(x) = \text{LCM} ((1 + x^5), (1 + x^3))$, where LCM stands for least common multiple. Reducing the degree of $R(x)$ is practically very important since this degree determines the number of parity bits. Reducing this number increases the efficiency of the scheme. Note that both $(1 + x^5)$ and $(1 + x^3)$ have $(x + 1)$ as a common factor. The polynomial $(1 + x^5)\cdot(1 + x^3)/(x+1) = (1 + x + x^2 + x^5 + x^6 + x^7)$ is then still divisible by both $(1 + x^5)$ and $(1 + x^3)$ and can therefore also be a suitable generating polynomial for our code. This simple observation already enables us to save one parity bit and to add an extra information bit instead. More than that, our code uses code words of length 15 for reasons given in detail in chapter 5. This is the value of Pu for the polynomial $(1 + x^5)\cdot(1 + x^3)$ $/(x+1)$, explaining why the code generated by this polynomial is cyclic. (The value of Pu for the polynomial $(1 + x^5)\cdot(1 + x^3)$ is 27.)

The above considerations apply generally to any t burst error-correcting code of the type treated in sections 5.8 and 5.9, whose code words should be divisible by $(1+x^{2t-1})$ and by $(1+x^t)$.

A.5.2   The Features of a Cyclic Code as Reflected from the Parity of the Number of Nonzero Coefficients in Its Generating Polynomial

The following statement was proved in section 5.9. Let **C** be a code generated by an LFSR R1, where the number of stages in R1, into which the feedback line is fed, is odd. Then all the code words of **C** have an even number of 1's.

This statement led to Conclusion 5.4 which indicated that it is always possible to detect the existence of an odd number of errors occurring in a code word of the code **C**.

An LFSR having an odd number of stages into which the feedback line is fed corresponds to a polynomial having an *even* number of nonzero coefficients. This is because the stages into which the feedback line is fed correspond to the polynomial's coefficients, except for the coefficient with the highest degree, which is always nonzero. This last coefficient represents the *output* line from the rightmost stage, as can be clarified by observing any LFSR and its corresponding polynomial treated in this chapter. The following proposition will be proved, for tutorial purposes, from polynomial considerations (although the discussion preceding Conclusion 5.4, and which states the same result, is easier and more obvious).

Proposition A.5 The code words generated by the polynomial $R(x)$, that has an even number of nonzero coefficients, all have an even number of 1 elements.

Proof One of the basic theorems in algebra states that if A is a root of a polynomial $R(x)$, then $R(x)$ is divisible by the polynomial $(x - A)$. In our case A can only have the value 0 or 1 and since we deal with a XOR operation, "−" is replaced by "+".

Take now a polynomial $R(x)$, having an even number of nonzero coefficients. For example, $R(x) = 1 + x^3 + x^5 + x^6$. Substituting the value 1 for x , we get $R(1) = 1 + 1 + 1 + 1 = 0$. That is, 1 is a root of $R(x)$, and it follows that $R(x)$ is divisible by $(x+1)$. The same applies for any $R(x)$ having an even number of nonzero coefficients.

The reverse argument is also true: namely, if a polynomial is divisible by $(x+1)$, then it has an even number of nonzero coefficients. The proof follows the same lines as above.

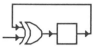

Fig. A.7 The LFSR corresponding to (x+1)

We continue the proof of the proposition by observing that if R(x) is the generating polynomial of a code then every code word V(x) is divisible by R(x). If R(x) has an even number of nonzero coefficients, then it is divisible by (x+1). The code word V(x) is therefore also divisible by (x+1) and therefore has an even number of nonzero coefficients, which completes the proof of Proposition A.5.

It is advisable to show the fact that if a polynomial V(x) is divisible by (x+1), then V(x) has an even number of nonzero coefficients, from a hardware point of view. The LFSR depicted in Fig. A.7 corresponds to the polynomial (x+1).

The fact that V(x) is divisible by (x+1) means that if V(x) is shifted into the LFSR depicted in Fig. A.7, the final contents of the register will be 0. On the other hand, it is clear that the functioning of this register is nothing but summing all the bits entering it. In other words, the fact that V(x) is divisible by (x+1) means that the sum of its coefficients is 0. That is, V(x) has an even number of nonzero coefficients.

We now treat the case where the generating polynomial of a code has an odd number of nonzero coefficients. (This case is less important than the one above but is quite interesting.)

Proposition A.6 A cyclic code whose generating polynomial R(x) has an odd number of nonzero coefficients has the property that the complement of a code word is also a code word.

Clarifying Remark Since very often we gave the name "cyclic code" to any code generated by a polynomial R(x), it should be stated that here the concept "cyclic code" means that the code is cyclic in the full sense of the word. That is, a cyclic shift of a code word is also a code word. In view of Proposition A.4, this means that $(1 + x^n)$ is divisible by R(x) (where n is the length of a code word), a property that will be used in the proof.

Proof Let I denote the "all 1" vector whose length n equals that of a code word in our code. Let $\underline{V}$ denote the complement of a code word V. We then have that $\underline{V} = V + I$. As our code is linear, we can prove that $\underline{V}$ is a code word by showing that I is a code word. This is shown as follows: a basic identity that is proved by a simple check is $(1 + x^n) = (1 + x) \cdot I(x)$, where I(x) is the polynomial corresponding to I. That is, it is a polynomial of degree $n - 1$ having nonzero coefficients for all x^i, $i = 0, 1, ..., n - 1$ (e.g., for n=4, $I(x) = (1 + x + x^2 + x^3)$). Since $(1 + x^n)$ is divisible by R(x), where n is the length of a code word (see the preceding clarifying remark), it follows that $(1 + x) \cdot I(x)$ is divisible by R(x). Since $(1+x)$ is not a factor of R(x) (R(x) has an odd number of coefficients), it follows that I(x) is divisible by R(x). That is, I(x) is a code word. This completes the proof of Proposition A.6.

Let us see how the property that the "all 1" vector I is a code word of a code is reflected in terms of the parity matrix T of the code. If I is a code word, then $I \cdot T = 0$. Multiplying T by I actually means here adding all the rows of T. Since this operation yields the 0 vector, this means that *each column of T has an even number of 1's.* We can conclude that if the generating polynomial of a cyclic code has an odd number of nonzero coefficients, then each of the columns of the parity matrix of the code has an even number of 1 elements.

A.5.3 Burst Error Detection

The following was considered and proved in sections 5.10 and 5.11: let C be a Hamming code generated by a register R of length n. (This LFSR has then maximal periodicity in the sense that when loaded with any nonzero initial value, it shifts pass through all the possible $2^n - 1$ nonzero combinations before returning to the initial setting.) Let V be a code word of C, and let V_j^B denote a vector obtained by introducing into V a burst error of length n whose pattern is B, where the burst starts at place j counting from the left. (The first place is 0.) If the burst pattern B is somehow known, then the following procedure for recovering j out of V_j^B applies. After loading V_j^B into R, keep shifting until R contains the burst pattern. If the additional number of shifts is k, then $j = 2^n - 1 - k$. We also noted that this observation validates the single error correction procedure of a Hamming code, in which case the 'burst" pattern is of the form (1000 ... 0).

   We now interpret the above, using polynomial terminology.

1. Expressing V_j^B in a polynomial form: B(x) is the polynomial representation of B. Multiplying B(x) by x^j moves the burst pattern to the j-th place along V, and the addition $V(x) + x^j \cdot B(x)$ inserts the errors into V. We then have $V_j^B(x) = V(x) + x^j \cdot B(x)$.

2. *Loading V_j^B into R:* The contents of R, after loading V_j^B into it, is $V_j^B(x) \bmod R(x)$.

3. *The recovery of j, based on k:* Shifting R after it already contains $V_j^B(x) \bmod R(x)$ means successive multiplications by x. The contents of the register after k shifts, starting with the contents $V_j^B(x) \bmod R(x)$, is then $[x^k \cdot V_j^B(x)] \bmod R(x)$. The statement regarding the recovery of j, based on the knowledge of k, means the following:

Proposition A.7   If there is a k such that $[x^k \cdot V_j^B(x)] \bmod R(x) = B(x)$, then $j = 2^n - 1 - k$.

This proposition has already been proved in chapter 5. It will now be proved again very simply, using polynomial arithmetic.

Proof Observe that:
$$V_j^B(x) \bmod R(x) = [V(x) + x^j \cdot B(x)] \bmod R(x)$$

It follows that:
$$[x^k \cdot V_j^B(x)] \bmod R(x) = [x^k \cdot V(x) + x^{j+k} \cdot B(x)] \bmod R(x) =$$
$$[x^k \cdot V(x)] \bmod R(x) + [x^{j+k} \cdot B(x)] \bmod R(x).$$

Obviously $[x^k \cdot V(x)] \bmod R(x) = 0$ since V is a code word. We then have that:
$$[x^k \cdot V_j^B(x)] \bmod R(x) = [x^{j+k} \cdot B(x)] \bmod R(x)$$

In order to prove the proposition, we have then to show that if there is a k such that $[x^{j+k} \cdot B(x)]$ mod $R(x) = B(x)$, then $j = 2^n - 1 - k$. This last statement is obviously true due to the maximal periodicity of R. (If R did not have maximal periodicity, we could find a value $m < 2^n - 1$ such that $j+k = m$, and still have $[x^{j+k} \cdot B(x)]$ mod $R(x) = B(x)$.)

This completes the proof of Proposition A.7.

It should be clarified that the proof above did not make any use of the fact that R has maximal periodicity. Proposition A.7 and the proof following it could be repeated word by word for any general case where the value $2^n - 1$ is replaced by Pu. Note, however, that Proposition A.7 starts with the words "*if* there is a k ...". There is no guarantee that for *any* B(x) of degree $n - 1$ or less there is a k such that $[x^k \cdot V_j B(x)]$ mod $R(x) = B(x)$, unless $Pu = 2^n - 1$. This is because only maximal periodicity R passes through all the possible forms of B(x).

A.6 A Formal Treatment of the Single-Character Correction RS Code

Introductory Remark   A single-character correction RS code was defined in chapter 5 as a code whose code words are blocks of $2^n - 1$ characters, where each character is of length n. The number of information characters is $2^n - 3$. Two parity characters enable the correction of a single - character error occurring during the transmission. The polynomial arithmetic aspects of this code are given in this section. The importance of the mathematical tools introduced here goes much beyond the specific application of RS codes, since they form the basis of a wide range of codes.

A.6.1 The Finite Field GF(q)

A **field** is a set of elements that define among themselves two operations, denoted by + and by ·. The set should be closed in the sense that if any of these operations is performed between two elements of the set, the result should also be in the set. Among the elements of the set there should be two, denoted by **0** and **1**, having the property that for every element x in the set there are in the set two elements denoted by $(-x)$ and by x^{-1}, where $x + (-x) = 0$, and $x \cdot x^{-1} = 1$. These operations should not necessarily be the ones known to us from elementary school. A **finite field** is a field with a finite number of elements.

The elements of **the finite field GF(q)** consist of the integers 0, 1, ... , q – 1 for a prime q. The + and · operations are the customary addition and multiplication operations, performed modulo q.

Example The elements of GF(5) are the numbers (0, 1, 2, 3, 4), where 1+2=3, 3+4=2, 2·4=3. The element (-1) is the element 4 since 1+4=0. The element 2^{-1} is 3 since 2·3=1.

Every GF(q) has a **primitive element** α such that every field element except 0 is expressed by some power of α (modulo q). Also, $\alpha^{q-1} = 1$. That is, operations in the exponent of α are performed modulo q – 1. (This last property holds for every field element.)

Without getting involved too much in number theory, we point out that the existence of α follows from the primality of q. Note, on the other hand, that the existence of the multiplicative inverse x^{-1} of any element x from GF(q), which is part of the definition of a field, is ensured by the existence of α. This is because there is a k such

that $\alpha^k = x$. We then have that $x^{-1} = \alpha^{-k} = \alpha^{q-k-1}$. All the operations are done, of course, modulo q.

An interesting field is GF(2). (2 is a prime number!) This field has only the two elements 0 and 1. By definition, additions are done modulo 2. That is, 0+0=0, 0+1=1, 1+0=0, 1+1=0. Note: *this kind of addition is exactly an XOR operation.*

A.6.2 The Field GF(2^n)

Definition **GF(2^n)** is a finite field whose elements are all the 2^n polynomials of degree $n - 1$ or less, with binary coefficients.

Two field elements of GF(2^n) are added similar to the way the code words of cyclic codes are added (these also are polynomials). Like the number q, in the case of GF(q), we have to define for the field GF(2^n) a term, modulo on which the multiplication operations of the field are performed. This term will be in our case a polynomial of degree n.

Definition The polynomial g(x) of degree n, modulo on which the operations of the field GF(2^n) are performed, is called **the generating polynomial of the field.**

Not every polynomial of degree n can be the generating polynomial of $GF(2^n)$. We need here a property identical to the primality of q. As discussed before, this property ensures the existence of a primitive element α whose powers generate all the elements of the field, except 0. Concerning our generating polynomial $g(x)$, we want there to be a polynomial α of degree $n-1$ or less, such that successive powers of α, when taken modulo $g(\alpha)$, will generate all the polynomials of degree $n-1$ or less, except for the "all 0" polynomial.

The last statement concerning the required property of $g(x)$ reminds us of a maximum periodicity LFSR and its corresponding polynomial $R(x)$. Observe again Proposition A.2 and Table A.1 following it. We see that all the powers of x between 0 and 6 yield different results, when taken modulo $R(x) = 1 + x + x^3$. This $R(x)$ can be the generating polynomial of $GF(2^3)$.

In order to clarify the argument above, let us generate polynomials of degree 2 or less, by exponentiating the term α, modulo the polynomial $g(\alpha) = 1 + \alpha + \alpha^3$, as listed in Table A.2.

Column (a) in Table A.2 lists successive powers of α, calculated mod $g(\alpha) = 1 + \alpha + \alpha^3$. That is, α^3 is always replaced by $1+\alpha$. It is clearly observed that powers of α generate all the elements of the field $GF(2^3)$, except for the 'all 0" polynomial. This means that $g(x) = 1 + x + x^3$ can serve as the generating polynomial of $GF(2^3)$. Column (c) in Table A.2

Mod $1 + \alpha + \alpha^3$		binary	Mod $1 + \alpha^2 + \alpha^4$
$\alpha^0 =$	1	(100)	1
$\alpha^1 =$	α	(010)	α
$\alpha^2 =$	α^2	(001)	α^2
$\alpha^3 =$	$1 + \alpha$	(110)	α^3
$\alpha^4 =$	$\alpha + \alpha^2$	(011)	$1 + \alpha^2$
$\alpha^5 =$	$1 + \alpha + \alpha^2$	(111)	$\alpha + \alpha^3$
$\alpha^6 =$	$1 + \alpha^2$	(101)	1
$\alpha^7 =$	1	(100)	α
etc.			
	(a)	(b)	(c)

Table A.2   Powers of α modulo $(1 + \alpha + \alpha^3)$ and modulo $(1 + \alpha^2 + \alpha^4)$

lists powers of α taken modulo the polynomial $g(\alpha) = 1 + \alpha^2 + \alpha^4$, where α^4 is replaced constantly by $1 + \alpha^2$. It is observed that $\alpha^6 = \alpha^0$, and the polynomial $g(x) = 1 + x^2 + x^4$ cannot generate the elements of the field $GF(2^4)$. Column (b) lists a short way of expressing the polynomials of column (a), where the polynomial is represented by a binary vector consisting of the polynomial's coefficients. Note that columns (a) and (b) are actually a repetition of Table A.1, using a different wording.

The field element α is *a polynomial*, and all the field elements are expressed as polynomials in α. In many cases, instead of expressing a certain field element y as a polynomial in α, we prefer to name y after the power of α that generates y (in the case where this power is known). For example take $GF(2^3)$ generated by $g(x) = 1 + x + x^3$. The field element $(1 + \alpha + \alpha^2)$ can be named α^5.

It should also be observed that exponentiating α modulo a polynomial $g(\alpha)$ means that α is a root of $g(x)$, in the sense that $g(\alpha) = 0$. This statement is self-explanatory, since operating modulo $g(\alpha)$ means that $g(\alpha) = 0$. However, for clarification purposes we prove this statement in more detail. Express $g(x)$ as $f(x) + x^n$. $f(x)$ is of degree $n - 1$ or less. Its coefficients consist of the $n - 1$ least significant coefficients of $g(x)$. (Note that the term x^n appears in $g(x)$, since we know that its degree is n. For example, $1 + x + x^3 = f(x) + x^3$ where $f(x) = 1+x$.) We then have $g(\alpha) = f(\alpha) + \alpha^n$. The fact that α is exponentiated modulo $g(\alpha)$ means that α^n is replaced by $f(\alpha)$. In other words, $\alpha^n = f(\alpha)$. (E.g., in the generation of column (a) of Table A.2, $\alpha^3 = 1 + \alpha$). If $\alpha^n = f(\alpha)$, then $g(\alpha) = \alpha^n + f(\alpha) = 0$, which proves the above statement.

Definition A polynomial $g(x)$ of degree n, with a root α, is called **a primitive polynomial** if α^i, when represented as polynomials in α of degree $n - 1$ or less, are different for $0 \leq i \leq 2^n - 2$.

By definition it follows that a primitive polynomial of degree n is the generating polynomial of $GF(2^n)$.

A polynomial of degree n has n roots (not all are necessarily different).

It is advisable to point out the other roots of the generating polynomial of $GF(2^n)$ beside α. This is done in Proposition A.8.

Proposition A.8 If α is a root of the primitive polynomial $g(x)$, then the other roots of $g(x)$ are α^{2^i}, $i = 1, 2, n - 1$.

Proof The square of a polynomial expression equals the sum of the squares of its terms plus twice all the possible products of two terms. For example, $(a + bx + cx^2)^2 = a^2 + b^2x^2 + c^2x^4 + 2(abx + acx^2 + bcx^3)$. In the case where the coefficients a, b, c are binary (that means that $a^2=a$, $b^2=b$, $c^2=c$), and the addition operation is XOR (that means that taking a term twice always yields 0), we have that $(a + bx + cx^2)^2 = a + bx^2 + cx^4$. It follows that in the cases treated in this section, $[g(\alpha)]^2 = g(\alpha^2)$. If α is a root of $g(x)$ then $g(\alpha) = 0$, and $[g(\alpha)]^2 = 0$. It then follows that $g(\alpha^2) = 0$; that is, α^2 is a root of $g(x)$. If α^2 is a root of $g(x)$, then its square α^4 is also a root of $g(x)$, and it then follows that α^{2^i}, $i = 1, 2, n - 1$, are all roots of $g(x)$. The indexing of i stops at $n - 1$ since operations in the exponent of α are performed modulo $2^n - 1$, meaning that $\alpha^{2^n} = \alpha$.

A.6.3   A Formal Treatment of a Single Character Correction RS Code

Based on the experience we have gathered so far, we understand the association between polynomials and code words of cyclic codes. Our RS code is also cyclic. It is generated by an LFSR (depicted in Fig. 5.15), and there is a generating polynomial associated with it.

Definition The **code word of an RS code** is a polynomial whose coefficients are elements from $GF(2^n)$.

Example Take the message M = (100, 001, 011, 101, 110, 111, 010), treated in section 5.13. The characters here are considered to be elements from $GF(2^3)$. They appear in column (b) of Table A.2, where column (a) lists the powers of α associated with them. We then have:

$$M(x) = (\alpha^0 + \alpha^2 x + \alpha^4 x^2 + \alpha^6 x^3 + \alpha^3 x^4 + \alpha^5 x^5 + \alpha^2 x^6).$$ (If one of the characters had been a zero, in which case there would not be a power of α associated with it, the character would have remained a coefficient of value 0.)

The RS code is actually an extension of the idea of cyclic codes to which we were used. Whereas the code words of the ordinary cyclic codes had coefficients from $GF(2)$, the RS code has coefficients from $GF(2^n)$, for n>1.

The association between polynomials and LFSR's is derived here in the same way it was done for $GF(2)$, where the polynomial's coefficients were determined according to the feedback connection of the LFSR. However, in our extended case the feedback connections of an LFSR also carry a nonbinary weight, and this weight should appear in the coefficients of the corresponding polynomial.

Example   Take the registers of the syndrome generators of Fig. 5.13, redrawn in Fig. A.8. Recalling the properties of the matrix Q, we note that if the character fed back in register #1 is the field element α^i, then

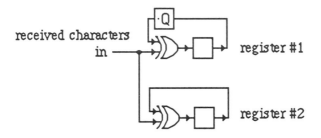

Fig. A.8: Fig. 5.13. redrawn

after multiplication by Q, its value becomes α^{i+1}. That is, multiplication by Q is equivalent to multiplication by α, and the feedback line has the "weight" α. The polynomial that corresponds to register #1 is then (α + x). The polynomial that corresponds to register #2 is (1 + x).

A code word of our RS code is characterized by the fact that it is divisible by both (α + x) and (1 + x). These polynomials are relatively prime, and the generating polynomial of our code is therefore $f(x) = (\alpha +$ x) $\cdot$ (1 + x) $= \alpha + (1+ \alpha)x + x^2$. This is exactly the polynomial corresponding to the register depicted in Fig. 5.15, where the operation of the matrix P is equivalent to the multiplication of the field element α^i (that is fed back from the rightmost stage) by (1+ α). All the code words of our code are then divisible by f(x) $= \alpha + (1+ \alpha)x + x^2$.

We now consider the effect of a single-character error inserted into a code word. In the case of the Hamming code the effect of a single error in place #i means adding the polynomial $1 \cdot x^i$ to a code word, where the 1, that was introduced here artificially, indicates the error "pattern". This pattern is from the field GF(2). With an RS code, the character error pattern is an element α^i of GF(2^n) (for characters of length n.) Inserting this error pattern into place #j of a code word (the characters are counted from the left, where the leftmost place is #0) means adding the polynomial $\alpha^i \cdot x^j$ to the polynomial representation of the code word.

Example Take the case of the message M' from section 5.13. It was obtained by inserting the character error pattern (001) into place #4 of a code word. If our RS code is based on the field GF(2^3), introduced in columns (a) and (b) of Table A.2, then $M'(x) = M(x) + \alpha^2 x^4$.

In order to clarify the mathematical interpretation of shifting a received message into the syndrome generators of Fig. 5.13, we use the specific case of M' shown above. Shifting M' into register #1 means dividing by $(\alpha + x)$. Since M is a code word, then $M'(x) \bmod (\alpha + x) = \alpha^2 x^4 \bmod (\alpha + x)$. Let us see in detail the division of $\alpha^2 x^4$ by $(x + \alpha)$. We start by dividing $\alpha^2 x^4$ by x. The first term of the quotient will then be $\alpha^2 x^3$. We then multiply $\alpha^2 x^3$ by $(x + \alpha)$, getting $\alpha^2 x^4 + \alpha^3 x^3$. This is added to $\alpha^2 x^4$, and the process continues. The entire operation is listed next: (The * notations are explained later.)

$* \alpha^2 x^4 \qquad\qquad : \quad (x + \alpha) = \alpha^2 x^3 + \alpha^3 x^2 + \alpha^4 x + \alpha^5$

$\quad \alpha^2 x^4 + \alpha^3 x^3$

——————

$* \alpha^3 x^3$

$\quad \alpha^3 x^3 + \alpha^4 x^2$

——————

$* \alpha^4 x^2$

$\quad \alpha^4 x^2 + \alpha^5 x$

——————

$* \alpha^5 x$

$\quad \alpha^5 x + \alpha^6$

——————

$* \alpha^6 \qquad$ remainder

Observing the intermediate results denoted by $*$, we reach the following conclusion: When dividing the term $\alpha^i x^j$ by (x + α), we perform successive steps of decreasing the power of x by 1, and increasing the power of α by 1. The sum of the powers of x and α after each step is therefore constantly i+j. The process terminates when we get the remainder α^{i+j}. We actually have here two counters working in parallel. One is an up-counter and the other a down-counter. For the specific case of our message M' we have M'(x) mod (α + x) = α^6.

Shifting M' into register #2 means dividing by (1 + x). Since M is a code word, then M'(x) mod (1 + x) = $\alpha^2 x^4$ mod (1 + x). It is simple to show that dividing $\alpha^i x^j$ by (1 + x) means successive reductions of the power of x, until we get the remainder α^i, that is the character error pattern. In our case the remainder is α^2.

After getting α^{i+j} and α^i from the two syndrome generators, we excute the process of recovering the value of j (that is the location of the erroneous character), as described in section 5.13.

INDEX

The MIT Press, with Peter Denning, general consulting editor, and Brian Randell, European consulting editor, publishes computer science books in the following series:

ACM Doctoral Dissertation Award and Distinguished Dissertation Series

Artificial Intelligence, Patrick Winston and Michael Brady, editors

Charles Babbage Institute Reprint Series for the History of Computing, Martin Campbell-Kelly, editor

Computer Systems, Herb Schwetman, editor

Exploring with Logo, E. Paul Goldenberg, editor

Foundations of Computing, Michael Garey and Albert Meyer, editors

History of Computing, I. Bernard Cohen and William Aspray, editors

Information Systems, Michael Lesk, editor

Logic Programming, Ehud Shapiro, editor; Fernando Pereira, Koichi Furukawa, and D. H. D. Warren, associate editors

The MIT Electrical Engineering and Computer Science Series

Scientific Computation, Dennis Gannon, editor